GOD ON ASSIGNMENT AS YOU

The True Story of Your Incarnation

David Hulse, D.D.

authorHOUSE®

AuthorHouse™ LLC
1663 Liberty Drive
Bloomington, IN 47403
www.authorhouse.com
Phone: 1-800-839-8640

Published by AuthorHouse   09/20/2013

ISBN: 978-1-4817-0167-9 (sc)
ISBN: 978-1-4817-0166-2 (e)

Library of Congress Control Number: 2012924088

"Is it not written in your law,
I said, you are gods?"
Jn. 10:34

DEDICATION

This book is dedicated to you the reader, who has opened your heart enough to becoming enlightened to your own true identity.

CONTENTS

ACKNOWLEDGMENTS

TAKING THIS BOOK, which started in the form of several booklets, and turning it into one book, has truly been an experience in community. My grateful thanks and appreciation to so many for the many hours spent in the preparation of this book.

My thanks to Brenda Dupuy – Peterson for editing and transcribing these tapes and messages to printed form.

The following "light workers" assisted in editing, proof-reading, and/ or feedback: Rebecca McCormick, Carla Reed and Aimee de Renouard. My appreciation to all.

My appreciation also goes to Tim Leach for making all the changes in the computer and for preparing the book for printing.

My grateful appreciation to each of the above for being part of this project!
Sincerely,
David

PREFACE

I REALIZE THAT this book may not be for everyone at this time. However, it is necessary to challenge the sensibilities of man-made traditions, which have made the word of present truth of no effect to this generation. I invite you to listen to your own inner Christ intelligence which is able to lead you to your truth, rather than listening to the feeble attempts of dogmatic voices that are only plunging us into the depths of unanswered questions.

In this day, there are several versions of the Bible. I suggest choosing the version which best suits your understanding of language. II Timothy 2:15 KJV says: Study to show thyself approved unto God, a workman that needeth not to be ashamed, rightly dividing the word of truth. The study presented in this book is based on the "Thompson Chain-Reference Bible", "Strong's Exhaustive Concordance of the Bible", the guidance of the inner teacher – the Holy Spirit, and spiritual *common sense*. The result has challenged much of the second-handed information that has been passed down through Christian patriarchy. This scripture also mentions, "rightly dividing the word of truth". To do this, we need to discern which scriptures are inspired by God and which scriptures contain man's perceptions and hidden political and cultural agendas.

All scripture *is* given by inspiration of God, and *is* profitable for doctrine, for reproof, for correction, for instruction in righteousness. (II Timothy 3:16 KJV)

The Greek lexicon shows us that translators omitted a comma after the word scripture and added the word *is* in the King James Version. Therefore, the scripture should read, in its proper context, "All scripture, given by inspiration of God and profitable for doctrine . . . ." It is important to note that italicized words indicate that the translators or KJV have added them.

Western religious thought has put a great emphasis on the masculinity of God. For the sake of language and the flow of reading, the pages that follow mostly address God in the masculine form. However, I honor and acknowledge the Goddess/Mother aspect of deity, (as shown in the name El Shaddai, the large and many-breasted one) that I equally celebrate in spirit.

If you are in the process of re-examining old childhood beliefs and have realized there has to be a "more excellent way," this book is for you. With this in mind, I invite you to open your minds and your hearts to this great process of incarnation, when an adventurous playful Creator chose to experience and play the game of humanity with all of its diversity.

My premise is that a Creator could not create anything less than itself as that would result in pity. Creating anything greater than itself would result in admiration. Only creating that which is equal results in love! You are the creator experiencing the richness of this human journey. You are god on assignment!

Author

PARANOIA  PROCESS

ANATOMY OF THE PROCESS

IF YOU SEEM to be going through a time of mistrust, disorganized thinking, and re-evaluation of beliefs, you could very well be experiencing the paranoia process. What is this process, and why must we pass through this dark upheaval on our way to at-one-ment?

In answer to that, I want to begin with a little background concerning the development of words so we understand the evolution of the meaning of this process.

Like everything else, the meanings of words have, through the passage of time, taken on completely different meanings from their original form. As their meanings change, many words have to be redefined.

The word *radical* is a great example of a word that has changed meaning over time. Today, it means a person who is radical is someone who has extreme politics to carry out their violent agendas. That's not what the word *radical* meant when it came into the English language from the Latin word *radix*. It's from that Latin word *radix* that we get the English word *radish*, because the word *radix* in Latin means root. We named the vegetable a *radish*, because it's a root/tuber plant.

In its original meaning, a *radical* is a person who wants to get to the root of things. It is someone who doesn't judge by appearances or by actions and effects, but is a person who says, "I know you did that, but

1

before I judge it, I'd like to understand why you did that." Jesus must have been radical, because He taught," Put the axe to the root of the tree." If that's being radical, I too want to be radical. In this sense, *radical* carries a higher, more positive meaning than what it has come to mean today.

Now, let's look at the word *religion*. It can be divided into two parts, the prefix *re*—and the rest of the word—*ligion*. The prefix *re*—suggests the action of going back or doing something again. *Webster's New World Dictionary* derives the word *religion* from the Latin word *religio* meaning the sense of right, or scruples, or religion. However, it is the root of *religio* that is of greater interest. *Religio* comes from the word *religare*, which means to bind back. The word *religare* is a combination of two words: *re*—which we know means going back or doing again and—*ligare* is to bind. We can see from this, the word *religion* carries the meaning to bind back or to bind again.

Yoke is another word that has been translated to mean "to harness or bind" by those who are believers in the literalism of the Bible. *Yoke*, however, as translated from the Aramaic as well as Sanskrit, actually means to join (unite) – union with universal spirit. The word *yoke* is the same Greek word used for yoga. The literalist use of the word *yoke (to bind)*, is a digression from the word *yoga (to unite)*. *Yoga* has the definition of being joined. Feel the difference? There is harshness when you say *yoked together*, (bound together), but when you say *yoga*, (joined together), there is softness to it. It's like the joining in a marriage. When Jesus said, "Take My yoke upon you, and learn of Me . . ." I believe He was saying, join with Me and learn my way (process). Learn My *yoga* process that unites body, mind and spirit together again. "He who unites himself with the Lord is one spirit." (1 Cor. 6:17 KJV)

However, religion came along and took the meaning of *yoga* (join together) and stepped it down to *yoke*, which means *bind together*. That is where the word *religion*, to bind again, has its origin. Isn't that what religion has done? Hasn't it BOUND together masses of people in consciousness through dogma?

PRECONCEIVED IDEAS

When I spoke about the word *yoga* recently, I could see the defensiveness of those listening. The people were thinking, "I didn't come here to hear about yoga! This is just too far out."

I don't know much about yoga, but I do see how people are captured by particular words. Some could not hear another thing I said because I used the eastern word *yoga*. Because of their preconceived definitions of yoga, they could not glean the understanding and truth contained in this word.

This is why some religious people become so difficult to communicate with, so defensive, so argumentative. It is very difficult to sit down and have an open-minded dialog. There is nothing, as far as they're concerned, to talk about. If you, in any way, present something a little new or different they take a defensive posture because it challenges their belief system.

Within religion, spiritual evolvement is not allowed to happen because the process is built upon a preconceived definition, or doctrine. Any time we delve into an area which we ourselves have not experienced yet try to define, it becomes detrimental to our spiritual progress. This is what the word *orthodox* means: conforming to established doctrine or opinion.

GIMME THAT OLD-TIME ORTHONOIA

Every person goes through three stages of consciousness on their way to understanding their Truth. The first stage is directly related to orthodox belief. This stage is called *Orthonoia*, which represents the state of mind of a commonly accepted set of external beliefs imposed upon a person. This is what we started believing because it is what our parents believed and it's what they taught us to believe. Orthodox consciousness is borrowed information. No one comes to these conclusions individually, through personal enlightenment. These conclusions are received from somebody else, as handed-down thinking. Because it references previous understanding instead of present experience, it is dead letter thinking.

Consider this: denominations are not built by millions individually enlightened people who have all come to a similar wonderful revelation.

In fact, great religions of the world can be traced to the revelation of one person like . . . . Mary Baker Eddy, Confucius, Mohammed, Joseph Smith or Martin Luther around whose personal revelation a denomination is built.

Do we understand that all denominations are built upon one person's *supposed* encounter with God? Certainly not every follower has experienced a similar encounter. Denominations were built on one person's experience, even though most of the people in those denominations today have never had the same experience. Most major religions in the world are traced back to one person. This is not to say that the people I've mentioned did not have valid spiritual revelation or some kind of experience beyond the natural. I've come to the conclusion that every one of them had a personal encounter with what we call the Divine, or else they could not be effective. One person cannot affect hundreds of millions of people without some type of a spiritual experience. Some spiritual revelations such as Islam, Buddhism and Catholicism have survived for thousands of years. A more recent example would be Swedenborg, an 18th century thinker from Sweden. Churches built on his teachings still exist as well as his books. People who still read and believe his writings are dedicated to them even though they've never met the man. There's got to be something to his teachings that resonates with some people's needs.

If I could sit down and talk to any one of the original thinkers about what their message has become, we would probably discover the current interpretation is not the same as their original experience because people have taken the founder's experience and organized it into a belief system.

Here's a little story I heard concerning the devil and a friend who were talking as they walked down the road one day. They looked up and saw a man bend down, pick something up and put it in his pocket. Nobody said anything at first, but finally, the friend said to the devil, "Did you see what that guy did?" The devil said, " Oh yeah, I saw him. He just picked up a piece of the truth." The friend replied, "Aren't you intimidated when somebody gets a hold of Truth?" Then the devil said, "No, I've learned if I leave them alone, they'll eventually organize it into a doctrine."

And that is exactly what has happened. The *devil* hasn't had to do a thing to anybody. People take truth and re-work it so that it can be organized to benefit their ego.

EXPERIENCE THE EXPERIENCE

As these men shared and radiated the light of their experience, people were drawn to them. However, if we could speak to those people, they would most likely say, "I did not mean for a religion to be built upon what happened to me. I wanted people to realize that what happened to me could happen to them. I wanted them to have the experience, not just a belief in *my* experience." They did not want the experience made into a mental construct that would become a religion. They wanted it to be kept as an experience that joined those who had the same experience.

However, people operating from their own ego watched the process realized revelation could become very powerful: economically, educationally, and socially. That's what that little story says to me about the devil and his friend. The devil doesn't have to do a thing with revelation. The carnal mind, which is the devil, will organize it.

In orthodox religion, wherever you start is most likely where you end up. The organizers don't tell us it is just a beginning. They leave us at the genesis of our journey and do not teach us how to find our individual path toward enlightenment.

THE INSANITY OF PARANOIA

After a person awakens from the orthonoia state of consciousness, the next experience is the state of *PARANOIA*. The dictionary defines this word as a condition in which the mind is disorganized and distrustful. This disarranged state questions the very basis of our psychic structure: our values, beliefs, perceptions and all desires and longings.

This is a difficult state to be in, for it's never easy to live in the darkness before the dawning of a new day. According to the scriptures, the new day started at sundown. That meant that a great part of the new day was under night time. Even in our time, we could say one minute after midnight is the beginning of a new day. If we wrote a check we'd have to date it the new day even though at that time there was no daylight. We've got to understand that we are starting out this new day while it still appears very dark upon this earth. What is going to make us strong in the new day is the time of darkness. Be very alert and understand that even though we know the new day is here and the new age is upon us, the masses of people are still not aware of it. The old ways will carry into the new and still be predominant for some time until the light of the sun appears. When the sun appears there will be a planetary awakening.

We're not talking about an exclusive bunch of people called born again Christians. I'm not putting that down, things had to be that way at first. God had to have people that were taken aside, that were exclusive or considered selected. That's where we get the word *church*. It's from a Greek word, *ekklesia*, which means the chosen ones, the called out. Don't settle for that state of consciousness. That's paradoxical. The whole thing of Israel being chosen and the church being chosen is paradoxical to this day. God went that direction first in order to have a people through whom He could reach all mankind. That's God's way. It's in the Bible in Acts 15. Paraphrased, it says:

1. God shall take out a people for His name's (nature) sake.
2. He shall build the tabernacle of David (new consciousness).
3. He will go back for the residue (rest of humanity) of mankind.

There are the three steps God uses to take people out of this *orthonoia*. That's where most of us came from. We came out of our orthodox beliefs. God said, "Come out of her. Be separate from her, My people. Be no more a partaker of her sins." We came out, and if you're like me, you've been in a state of total paranoia because you keep hearing a word that changes all the time, and you can't get settled.

The PARANOIA STATE IS A PROCESS of always evaluating and resetting priorities. It's a state where we begin to think and question what we've been taught from the past. Some people find this process difficult.

However, this is what builds the tabernacle and what establishes a people on the earth who are not at the level of the orthodox consciousness.

Experiencing this state of paranoia is crucial. Although our religious minds tell us that it is wrong for us to go through a period of disarranged or unclear thinking. It's important because if this is happening, you have begun to go back and look at the states of consciousness made of beliefs that have been imposed upon you.

Having been raised in the orthodox Pentecostal denomination, I was never once told that I had any rights to check out anything other than what they believed. Never did they feel secure enough in their own structure of belief and thinking about God for me to check out anybody else's beliefs. Did we ever have anyone that encouraged us to research or to look into other religions, or to check them out to see if other people were correct? No, we were told everything else was heresy, was erroneous or was the doctrine of the devil. If you questioned it, the judgments of God would fall upon your life. Now, where does that come from? It comes from the ego, the uncertainty, the erroneous mind which has been passed down. This kind of thinking is what is meant when the Bible says that the sins of the fathers have been visited upon many generations. Sin is not only an act, but sin is also a belief; and that belief is imposed upon and visited upon each generation until the blind lead the blind, and they all fall into the ditch. I admire everyone who possesses the courage to leave the orthonoic stage and travel on through the paranoia process.

PARANOIA IS POSITIVE

It seems that those who are presently in the paranoia state are questioning everything they've been told and believed. The beautiful thing about it is that truth cannot be lost. Truth just moves right along with us in our progression. You don't have to fear examining and re-evaluating or putting what you believe to the test. If it came from the Holy Spirit in us, it will stand up to scrutiny and qualify the test. You will not be overtaken by the adversary in this wilderness period, but will be moved into the next realm of your experience. If your belief system doesn't survive this test, it means that light has come and exposed beliefs not based in truth. So, be comfortable with this paranoia stage.

If it does not come from our own spiritual Divine Self, which is the image of God, it is not real. It does not come from the part of us that is reality, therefore it does not have a source in reality. How can anything be real that does not come from reality? For example, the earth appears flat, but now we know it's not flat. It is round. Any amount of belief in its being flat is simply not true. It will never be flat, no matter how much you believe it.

Finally, we end up at the *METANOIA* state. This state is interesting, because it's the word our Bible uses for repentance. It means a 'change of mind, or heart, or a new state of consciousnesses'. The church told us that repentance was going down to an altar and saying, "Jesus, I'm sorry." That isn't even what the word repentance meant when it entered the Bible. Those who taught us religious dogma told us that repentance meant to change what we did. They substituted an action in place of a change in consciousness.

THE METANOIA EXPERIENCE

Revelation alters thought and truth transforms thought. However, what we want is more than an altered state of consciousness. Changing our perception does require more than changing an old thought for a new thought. Metanoia is an experience that awakens new thought and renders old thought null and void.

Consider our economic system, for example. Experts say the greatest fear in our economy is not what happens with the stock market, but the way people perceive and respond to what happens. If people are scared because of a dip in the stock market and stop buying new cars and new houses, etc. they themselves, by their own actions, because of their own perceptions, will cause an economic crash in this country.

PEOPLE – not just a few politicians in Washington – are the CAUSE of what makes the economy work. The power is in the people's hands, not in the politicians' control. We've got it backwards. We are so blinded and so brainwashed that we've used a few politicians in Washington to be our scapegoat as to what's going on, therefore, as in everything else, we don't accept our responsibility. One of the things that will happen, in the brightness of the dawning of a new age on this planet, is that the power will be awakened in the people. The people will realize they are the ones who make the changes, not a few minorities who decide to think for the masses and manipulate them into what they want for themselves. It doesn't matter what politicians we vote into office: that's not where the change will happen. Change will not happen by changing laws. Laws are nothing. Laws are illusionary because they are formed as restrictions or rules to be imposed upon those who believe they are first a body instead of spirit.

We need to shift our perception. Any time we just replace an old thought with a new thought, we remain in a duality of mind. If you see an opposite from your present state of being, you are still in a double-mindedness. Realize, when we say one word, it keeps its opposite alive to fight and oppose it. The old will always fight the new. The new will always fight the old. Evil will always be against good, and good will always be against evil. There is no way that I can acknowledge good without acknowledging the existence of evil.

GROWING IN THE PROBLEM

These three stages, *orthonoia, paranoia,* and *metanoia,* remind me of something I taught years ago. I used to call it the three P's: the Promise, the Problem and the Provision. The subject concerned the children of Israel when they were in Egypt and God's promise to them of a land where milk and honey flowed. Finally, God grew tired of their remaining in Egypt with only a promise. Promises are great to a point, but a promise is exactly what it says—it's a promise of that which is to come. In the denomination in which I was raised we used to sing, "Standing, Standing, Standing on the Promises of God, Our Savior." And that's what a lot of us are still doing, standing on the promises—holding them down and KEEPING THEM PROMISES. Promises should become provisions.

If someone you love promises to come and have dinner with you, you might find that exciting and say, "Someone special is going to come over next Thursday at seven o' clock. I must prepare for it." But if they don't come, what good is the promise without the fulfillment? The promise itself only prepares us for something else to take place. In fact, without fulfillment, a promise can cause great disappointment.

Imagine the Israelites thinking, "God has promised us a land where milk and honey flows." They assumed when God brought them out of Egypt, they would move into the provision of that promise, but what they did not understand was before God would bring them from one state to another state, he had to bring them to a place of change. God never allows anyone to leave one realm and enter a new realm without growth. There is always some kind of a process where awareness, growth and evolution takes place.

What moves us to the next place in our lives is the fulfillment of a certain stage of growth where we are. Israel would have gone into Canaan in the same condition as they were when they lived in Egypt with only the promise. So between the promise and the provision,—God put the problem; the wilderness. We can stand in the promise and never grow, or we can make it to the provision and never have grown. Either we will grow in the problem, or we will stay in the problem. That first generation never understood God's process of preparing them to enter into the provision. They never changed their perception. They stayed rebellious, resisting the things of God until the entire generation died in the wilderness. God had to raise up a new generation.

FULLFILLING GENERATIONS OF CONSCIOUSNESS

Symbolically, these generations represent stages of consciousness through which we pass in our development. As long as we perceive our provision from an old perception, we can have all of the promises of life and immortality and heaven, or whatever our ultimate goal is, and still die in Egypt or in the wilderness with nothing but the promise.

Until our perception is changed to the level where we see ourselves entering into the land of promise, we cannot enter in. It wasn't God keeping Israel out. It was the Israelites themselves. We have this concept that God is out there with this timetable saying, "At a certain time we'll do this, and at a certain time that will be enough of that," but it doesn't work that way. These things happen when certain realms of consciousness are fulfilled in us.

THROUGH THE AGES

There is no way I can look at this world and say that the entire world (speaking of the cosmos) is living in the same age (or state of consciousness). There are people who live in the age of law and others who are in the age of grace simultaneously. Some are in the age of new technology, in the new age, in the end-time, or the dark ages. This is all happening at the same time on this earth. We need to realize the time we live in is a composite of many levels of our individual perspectives.

The people who see God as legalistic and as a God who is going to throw the book at them if they don't do things a certain way, are people who live and believe in the law. These people live in an age of law consciousness.

Other people who feel that the law has been fulfilled live in the grace and the mercies and the love of God. They live in the age of grace.

There are also people who believe we are in the end-times of the church age, which they define as seven years of tribulation when certain negative things are going to happen. Moreover, because they believe this way, they are a part of making these things happen. They read their newspapers and listen to the news every night and draw whatever they believe out of it. They pull these things out of the illusionary external world and make them real, and because they are saying, "I believe in that," it becomes real to them. This is what we call a self-fulfilled prophecy.

We can put ourselves into seven years of tribulation if we choose to believe that we've entered seven years of tribulation. Or we can change our whole perception and switch to the belief that we've already had forty years of tribulation and we don't need another seven years of it. We can

11

choose to believe we are in the millennial age of blessing and I believe we can draw that to us as well.

We choose this day "Whom" we will serve. Which consciousness will we make our reality?

THE DEEPER EXPERIENCE

We need to go deeper and experience a mysterious paradox which is: the more impersonal I get, the more inner-personal I become. When I came into the understanding of my spiritual identity I remember the first criticism I heard people say about me was that I thought I was better and spiritually superior. The truth was, I was feeling more humble when discovering my true authentic identity.

The minute we step outside the lines of traditional thinking, we intimidate people who react by saying things like, "Who do you think you are? What kind of a hotline do you have with God that I don't have?" If that happens in our lives, it is helpful to understand this paradox: when God separates us, it is only to bring things back together at a much deeper level and on a much larger scale.

For example, Jesus lived among the people as a physical being. They could talk to Him. They could look into His eyes. They could reach out and touch Him. Jesus said, "I have to go away. I have to leave." What they couldn't understand is why he had to leave at such a young age. However, Jesus understood that to actually get closer to all people, He had to leave his physical form and be transformed into a spiritual form. In physical form He could be WITH only a few; transformed into a spiritual form, He could be IN all.

Whenever something seems to be going backwards in our lives, we must understand that it is just God's springboard for something new, getting ready to take place, for the purpose of our spiritual evolution and expansion. For example, when shooting a rubber band across the room, we have to pull it back as far as we can in order to shoot it farther. Maybe, that's what we're feeling. When our life circumstances get pulled back, we think we will break. The truth is at the very moment we think we're going to break; we are thrust further along our path. Each time we surpass the place we started from, and go a little farther. The process of evolution is at work. The process of awareness is happening. The expansion of God is taking place.

EXPERIENCE FOR THE UNIVERSAL PURPOSE

Most likely what is happening to us collectively as a people mirrors what is happening to us individually. Anything that we are experiencing as part of a collective group is not to be taken so personally that it obscures the purpose of our individual experience to benefit the whole. What we are experiencing personally may be for the whole. Don't let yourself think, "This is just me going through this; this has nothing to do with anybody else. Nobody understands where I'm coming from."

The worst thing we can do is to go hide in a corner somewhere, pull the cover up over our heads and think it will all go away. The best thing we can do to shift our perception and say, "Wait a minute. I am not alone; I am part of the universal purpose on this earth to raise the consciousness of the whole planet." That purpose does not seem overwhelming to us if we are not yet awakened. We need to shift our minds immediately from believing that we are having an exclusive experience that nobody else in the world is going through to knowing it can work for our highest good and the benefit of all. How can we withhold from one another when we understand that if one suffers, at a deep level we all suffer, and when one rejoices, we all rejoice? It is because we are all connected to the network of a cosmic intelligence. A new atmosphere of thought is being authored on this planet.

GIVING THINGS POWER

Nobody is doing anything to me that I don't allow. I give people power by the way I interpret what they do and by the way I respond. Our Divine Intelligence knows everything we need and is drawing it right to us.

As challenging as it is to say, "God, I am willing to receive whatever it takes to awaken spiritually," this is how to pray more consciously. Rather than pray, "Oh, God, this is difficult, take it away!", our prayers should mature and become more like, "O, God, give me the strength to understand what it is You're speaking to me through this situation."

Don't run from your feelings. Meet them head on, and dive into them and say, "Okay, I'm going to experience you, instead of you experiencing me." Become acquainted with your feelings inside and out. You can't do that when you're running from your feelings. Stay present.

TRANSMUTING THE EXPERIENCE

When we shift our perception, we are able to experience a situation from a new level of understanding. The greatest conflict of our lives occurs when we meet a situation at the level where it was created. If we can allow the situation to come into the level of consciousness which we've attained, something happens to that experience. It may start out as a challenge but as it matures and transforms, the situation goes from one level of consciousness to another. Biblically, we would say it transforms from a sword into a plowshare. I've used that expression for years to explain the law of transmutation. God said to take the same swords that killed many young men, left many children without a father and many wives without a husband, and to beat them into plowshares in order to plow the fallow ground of the earth so it could bring forth seed and fruit to feed the people. My point is that at one level, the swords were destructive, but at another transformed level, they became constructive.

THE POWER OF AT-ONE-MENT

We must realize that the power to transmute any experience lies within us. That power is a power we share with God. We are not trying to obtain that birthright; it has already been given to us. It IS ours. We have a birthright that gives us complete access to all that God is.

I am not saying: "Although we are *gods* we are not all that God is". What I am saying is that we are created in the likeness of God. *We share the potential with God.* We share the attributes with God. We are not separate, dependent human beings that constantly have to look to a God outside ourselves. We can know and experience God in a union within ourselves, a union of the Father and the Son as one. "I in them and you in me, that they may become completely one." (John 17:23)

The idea of separation evolved through doctrines such as "the trinity," which was created by Roman Catholic Nicene councils of the fourth century. This doctrine was not taught in the church during the first and second century. The word *trinity* is not found in the King James Bible, but the ego uses it to keep itself protected by endorsing a belief of separation. If we see God as separate, we certainly can't see our own union with God. As long as the Father and the Son and the Holy Ghost are three separate entities, separate Gods, then it is easy to see how a belief in spirit, soul and body was derived from that premise. If God is Father, Son, and Holy Ghost; then I am spirit, soul, and body. However, if we shift our consciousness to one of unity (oneness) from the doctrine of trinity (separation), we can understand our own at-one-ment with all things. Let the middle wall of partition come down and understand the oneness of spirit, soul, and body. The only reason we see them as three is because of our belief. Change the belief! Shift the perception! Make the best out of wherever you are on your path with the intention of moving toward the fullness of your soul's purpose.

FINDING AT-ONE-MENT

Life is sometimes like people going to a football game. They come from different directions, different streets and different routes. Some come on a bus. Some people drive cars; Some walk. It is not important how people arrive as long as they get there. The way we choose to experience our journey—what vehicle we choose makes no difference to God. Just get there! Get moving! The point is to just start heading in the direction. Get out of complacency. "I'd rather you be hot or cold," saith the Lord. (Rev. 3:16) I'd rather see people doing something considered wrong than doing nothing at all, because sometimes by doing something wrong, that action can correct you. There's a wonderful scripture in Jeremiah 2:19 that says, "Thy wickedness shall correct thee." I can understand why God allows what we call wickedness. Sometimes people will never come to anything who don't do SOMETHING. That's what I think is being said there, *I'd rather you do something – anything, but if you are complacent, if you are lazy, if you go nowhere, you'll never learn anything, because you're hiding in your own comfort zone.* You've heard said, "an idle mind is the devil's playground." It's the truth.

RAISING OUR CONSCIOUSNESS

What will raise the consciousness of the world are minds that allow the very essence of truth and spirit to flow and move into many different ideas and concepts. My thoughts have moved through many arenas concerning Christ and numerous other matters.

One thing that I came to a revelation about is that Jesus Christ is the *soul* of God. Jesus Christ stepped down from spirit to become spirit at another frequency which we call the soul. "Let this mind be in you which was in Christ Jesus." (Philippians 2:5).

There have been ideas and words that we've been afraid of at one level, but don't have to be afraid of at another. For example, I'm not afraid of the idea of having a philosophy for life. What would this world be without a philosophy? I'm not talking about the philosophies of humankind. What if the Spirit wants to give us a philosophy? Can you imagine yourself without some point of view on how to view life? Of course not. The only thing I'm against is philosophies offered by the ego. Is not the Kingdom of God a philosophy? Isn't it the principle of life? Whether we want to admit it or not, that's really what's important. What we make of the next five minutes or the next hour is the most important thing we have right now. We need to focus on a Kingdom point of view and bring it down to let it transform where we live. God can move through people who are not worried, who are happy, much more easily than through people who are continually worried over finances, worried over this and worried over that. Worry seals the fountains and dams the flow of life itself.

POVERTY-CONSCIOUS RELIGION

Poverty–Conscious Religion has taught many of us to believe financial things are unimportant. For instance, I was taught that being poor was spiritual, and that to have anything was worldly. People were scared to dress nicely or to have a nice car, as everybody in the church thought we were backsliding. I hope we've raised our consciousness to get out of such erroneous thinking. There is a price to pay on one hand for enlightenment. Always remember that where much is given, much is required.

People ask me, "What must I do to get involved?" I can't answer that. It is not for me to tell you or to give you your direction. You must turn within yourself. Yet, I do realize being involved means getting involved from a level of spiritual consciousness rather than from a political, social or religious viewpoint. There is more that we can do through the Spirit right now to change this world.

God knows the human condition and where it lies, and God's grace is sufficient. Grace says, "I can understand where we are." However, let's not stay here. Let's grow and become people with more spiritual insight who are able to deal with problems at a different level than from the level at which the problems were made. The downfall of politics and society and everything else is because the same mind that made the problems is trying to solve the problems and this doesn't work. It's going to take a higher level of thinking to change.

There are some things that are habitual. They're mechanical. We've always done it that way; so we'll always do it that way. Our consciousness needs to be awakened enough to meet these patterns with an enlightened mind. When the darkness comes, the light doesn't fight the darkness.

When somebody calls us an unkind name, if we catch it at that split second, the Holy Spirit will work with us. He will teach us and lead us and guide us, but we must first think WITH the Holy Spirit. In other words, our ability to catch it in consciousness at that level gives the Holy Spirit the invitation to come in and to take over our nature. At that point, showing love becomes natural and not unnatural. It's unnatural for me to love somebody who just called me a dirty son-of-a-gun. Humans don't do that. Humans render evil for evil. Humans render an eye for an eye, a tooth for a tooth. If you're going to fight me, I'm going to fight you. That is just good old human thinking. That's the norm of human reactive behavior. I need to shift my perception to realize that I am on this earth to see God in everyone, to make God available to everyone at every level, in every situation.

I am of the reality that says, *I change not, I am the same yesterday, today, and forever.* I am not that part of myself which is moved by wrong thinking, which produces wrong feelings and emotions. That is the unreal part of me. That is the part that has taken its identity from the outer unreal world. Reality in the Kingdom of God is peace, love and righteousness.

SEEING GOD IN ALL THINGS

We must understand that our purpose on this planet is to see God in every person, in every situation. No matter how someone acts toward us, we do not have to react from their level, as they are reacting from the unreal part of themselves. Our obligation is to always act from our reality; therefore, no one can take our peace. No one, acting from the unreal part of their mind, can take our peace which demonstrates the reality that we are and have always been.

This does not require some formula or some tremendous amount of work. I am saying we need to be still and know God is God, and let this revelation work out of us. We don't have to work for it. We work OUT our salvation. We don't work FOR our salvation. We work OUT our salvation with fear and trembling. All I have to do to let my reality flow out of me is to be still. The only obligation I have in any situation is not to act on emotions based on what I have been taught from a world that is coming from its own unreality and from its own insanity. If I do, I'll act insanely. Insanity with insanity will breed more insanity. Rendering evil for evil breeds more evil. Those who hate, breed more hate. Fighting those who fight you will breed war. Remember what the scripture said about Jesus in John 14:30, "Coming to you, the adversary will find nothing IN you."

You say, "That's hard to do. If somebody's mad at me, my reaction is to be mad at them." Only when you shift your perception can you realize the person isn't being angry with you out of their reality. Their unreality manifests as their unreal self acting out. I'm to love the REALITY of that person that's doing this to me. So, why should I react to anything other than what they are in reality? If I'm coming from what I am, I'll treat you for what you are. If I'm coming from a part in me that I think I am, then it puts me on the same level from which you're treating me. Then, I will in turn, react from the same level that you are coming from rather than from the level of my own reality. Every time I react from the level in which you treated me, you and I are going nowhere. There isn't one thing happening with our relationship that is going to enlarge or expand our spiritual awareness until we both come from our own identity.

COMING FROM OUR TRUE IDENTITY

To act from our true identity, all we have to change is our perception. The only effort I see involved in this so-called miracle that's taking place is to realize we have a Christ mind in us which can perceive an unreal world and give it some real meaning. This is how we minister to other people. The best way we can minister to an unlovely person is out of our love, but we'll never help or minister to anybody who is unlovely by ministering to them out of our own un-lovingness.

People don't want to hear our scriptures. They want us to express our love through the lives we live. They want to be in somebody's presence who's coming from a whole different place than where they are. We can quote our scriptures about Jesus all we want to, but if we aren't in any different shape than they are, nobody's going to pay attention. They don't care what we're saying because they want truth ministered to them from the level of experience and not as an intellectual concept. This is what makes the difference. After that, we can sit down and give them our scriptures. Our experience witnesses to them as a demonstration of truth, an example of experience being made the word.

THE WORD MADE FLESH

When we bring our reality into our experience, that's the word being made flesh. We think the flesh will be made word, but it's our spirit reality (I AM) that makes the first move. We first give the word, which when acted upon, becomes a living word – the word made flesh. The ego cannot make the words we say come alive. It's the experience that does that. When we speak of something from the level of experience, I guarantee it becomes a living word.

That's why the Christians teach God manifested in the flesh to be called the Son of God, which was the word made flesh. The whole success of the gospel comes from the fact that God came and was made flesh, and experienced the flesh, but never left the spiritual state. God never lost the true identity of who he was in the human experience.

THE INDESTRUCTIBLE TRUTH

Jesus came to announce, "Let Me show you that Truth cannot die—it will resurrect *again!*" As in the Law of Thermodynamics, it states energy (spirit) cannot be destroyed but can only change form. It simply wasn't about his personality as a human being. It wasn't something historical for us to look back two thousand years ago and say, "Oh, how wonderful about Jesus." No, He was trying to show us that everything we truly are, in reality, no man can destroy. Just like energy, Truth cannot be threatened, and reality cannot be destroyed. The crucifixion was meant to show us that who we are cannot be killed. How many times have you ever said, "I don't think I can go through this one more time. I can't handle this one more time." But you did. What was it that got you through? It was your Reality that gave you the grace to find a way through life's challenges and bring you out of hopelessness. It will always bring us out of a state of complacency, because we cannot kill or crucify the Truth.

Jesus wasn't trying to do something supernaturally beyond us. He was showing us something that could be a reality in every one of our lives. As *A*

Course In Miracles states, "Reality cannot be threatened, therefore unreality does not exist. Herein lies the peace of God".

Don't we surprise ourselves sometimes, with what we can take and what we can handle, and how we are able to come out of it? We can give the glory to God—the God in us, the God we are, the God we are a part of.

Nothing stays in a death state. Nothing. We may think it's dead; we may perceive it as dead; we may believe it to be dead, but somewhere it will resurrect. It doesn't even make any difference about those who leave the physical realm. No one will ever find death as an absolute, as a final state. When it comes to the eternity of who and what we are, there is no death. That's what Jesus tried to show us. Go to the grave; let them hang us on the cross—they can't kill Truth. Truth always resurrects and comes forth.

BEING TRANSFORMED

We are at a level in this journey where we ought to be experiencing some changes in our lives. Transformation doesn't happen by itself; it happens by the renewing of our mind. The word *renewing* carries the same meaning as the word *remembering. Re-new. Re-member.* As soon as we can remember who we are, we will be joined together with the Lord (universal law). Religion will re-bind us, but the process Jesus said to learn will RE-JOIN us to our original state as spiritual beings. It happens by remembering that the mind is renewed, then transformation comes.

The next time we're caught in a human dream, and we think we're angry at somebody; we should pause to realize that we're not angry at somebody else. Sometimes we think we're angry at somebody else. Don't we end up really angrier at ourselves? I do. We say awful things; we act badly, but the next thing we know, it's not even somebody else with whom we're angry. Later, we say, "Oh I can't believe I acted like that." We are angry because they awakened the anger that was already present but unresolved in us.

We always come to this truth when we are at the end of a situation. If we can do it at the end, then why can't we do it at the beginning? Let's "let this mind be in you that was in Christ Jesus." Phil. 2:5. We don't

21

have to do anything or try to work at it. The next time a similar situation happens, we should go into immediate meditation, let our mind just shut off, and let this mind be in us which was in Christ Jesus. The next thing we know, we'll be totally acting from a different part of our mind, because we'll be thinking differently. We'll be thinking from adjusted thoughts, and we'll feel so wonderful when it's over because we didn't fall into the pit of human experience. Now, when this happens, we are transformed from our human experience into a new creation. All we did was to change the way we thought. We didn't change the person who made us angry. We didn't change the world. We didn't change anything but ourselves. That's what the Holy Spirit does.

THINKING WITH SPIRIT

Nothing is real in the outer world. The aspect of our inner world God has given us is called the Holy Spirit, Who, when invited, will move into the consciousness to adjust and align it. He always stands at the door and knocks and says, "Somebody, let Me in," but if we move into our old anger and our old thought patterns, the door is never opened.

How do we open the door? We must think with the Spirit. *I will help you, guide you, lead you, teach you, but you must think with Me.* That means all we have to do is adjust our thinking to understand the situation from the level of consciousness that the Spirit has brought to us. The minute that happens, the door opens, and the Holy Spirit comes in. What we will be doing now is not a self effort, but it is natural, because we will be acting by the Spirit through our true identity. At this point, our natural self has become spiritualized, and we will now be doing natural things from a spiritual level.

ACT FROM OUR REALITY

I don't want us to think that we do this through discipline. If we discipline the ego, it will mock love. In other words, I might act lovingly to someone without feeling very loving. Don't do that. That's religious.

Religion is a pretentious outward expression – for example, dressing a certain way to appear holy, or not doing certain things to express holiness. We can fool a lot of people and make them think we really are holy, but there's no holiness in it. Holiness comes from our identity within ourselves which understands that we are already whole and complete and at one with life. In other words, that we are God manifested.

God doesn't want actors. God wants people who give forth an availability to be the reality that flows into this outer world. We don't have to act for God, that would be mocking God. Just let God be God, and love will flow naturally because God loves the world.

OUR "NOW" CONSCIOUSNESS

We can't separate ourselves from God. We didn't get an idea separate from what God is. What God is, *is* the idea. We need to go down into the mental process and understand that the Spirit is becoming consciousness. God is NOW a consciousness. We're going to understand that by never leaving the Spirit level, God IS idea now. At one time I couldn't have said that, because the ideas we had came from the ego ABOUT God. Now the idea is coming from Spirit, and it IS God. Remember Jesus taught, "the words spoken to you are spirit and life". John 6:63. The prophets had a high level word ABOUT the spirit, but Jesus is the only one who said, "My words ARE spirit" (emphasis mine). We desire to get to the place where we can say our ideas ARE spirit. We don't want just good ideas *about* spiritual things. That only reinforces separation.

A Shift In Perception

A NEW FOCUS

SPIRITUAL AWAKENING BEGINS when we extend beyond individual boundaries and comfort zones to enter a broader awareness. A period of tremendous change and transition precedes our entry into a new era. Specific intimate issues of monumental value in building a new consciousness come to the forefront of awareness at this point of expansion. The teachers of the new era will be educators who will inform and instruct humankind in the dynamics of how to live in the new earth.

When shifting our perception, a new focal point is introduced, as old belief systems are reevaluated. This process produces a vital shift in perception. The magnitude of our power is our ability to make a different choice. However, we are often not aware of the choices available to us in the present moment. In other words, it is possible to be unaware of prayers that have already been answered. A shift in perception awakens one to discover that many things thought to be unattainable or absent from life, in reality, have been there all along. A miracle is a shift in perception. It is our perception that needs adjustment, not the external events of life. External events will adjust to the new perception.

Understanding the psychological process of thinking and how we believe is an essential part of experiencing a shift in perception. On the path of progressive thinking, a journey must be made into the psyche to discover and uncover the great mystery of why we are the individuals we are.

This chapter is directed to those who have been unable to find healing, miracles, and answers through the multitude of avenues presented by various religions, metaphysics, and social thinking. I speak to those who have explored the unending and disheartening task of seeking deliverance from ourselves. More accurately, the self that has been defined in terms of religion and society that made us believe we were less than what we were created to be.

What is a shift in perception? Webster defines the word *shift* as "a change of direction, place, or position." The word *perception* is defined as "a physical sensation interpreted in the light of experience; also, a capacity for comprehension." A shift in perception, therefore, gives us the ability to comprehend the physical sensations of love or hate, peace or turmoil, health or disease. It is this comprehension that enables us to change our viewpoint of life by changing the directions of our thoughts. When a shift in perception occurs, experiences once considered defeat can be seen as triumphs. Perhaps the most amazing result of a shift in perception is that all experiences of life can be viewed from a non-judgmental point of view, which creates peace in all situations. A mind that remains in a position of non-judgment is prepared for impregnation by the higher thoughts of spirit.

A journey into the psychological process of thinking is the beginning of a shift in perception.

REWRITING OUR LIFE SCRIPT

Since we have free will, we were endowed with the power to choose and create the conditions of our earthly experiences. We created the conditions seen on the earth today when we turned from the mind of spirit to the mind of E.G.O.

"And the Lord God formed man of the dust of the ground, and breathed

into his nostrils the BREATH OF LIFE; and man BECAME a living SOUL" (Gen. 2:7).

The Hebrew word for *breath* is *neshamah,* meaning "intellect, divine inspiration, soul, spirit." This is the "breath of life" God breathed into the person. It was Spirit expressing itself as soul, and they were one.

This Scripture goes on to say that the person BECAME, through a process of free-will, *a living soul.* This soul, which is different from the word *neshamah,* which means divine spirit soul, was breathed into mankind by God. A Living Soul in the Hebrew is *nephesh,* meaning "animal, bodily or mental, beast, desire, greed, lust, mortal." *Nephesh* **is not** the spirit-soul God breathed into us, but is the soul we became. We were given a spirit-soul, which contained both the ability and capacity to think and express higher thought through our free will. We, through the soul we became, began to think about the thoughts of the spirit-soul we had been given through the breath of life. A distorted perception was developed through this process and we became a different thinker. We became beings with a different point of view and a different kind of mindset. *Nephesh* is the mind that we BECAME, through a process, which appears adversarial to the reality of Spirit-mind.

"A double-minded person is unstable in all his ways." (Paraphrased, James 1:8) *Double* in the Greek is *dipsuchos* meaning, "two spirited, vacillating in opinion or purpose." Here we see the two perceptions — the spirit-soul mind God breathed into us *(neshama),* and the living soul *(nephash),* which we ourselves formed and became. The higher *(neshama)* spirit-soul mind breathed into us was soon forgotten, lying dormant under the mirage of counterfeit expressions and experiences produced by the *nephesh* soul we became.

Many areas of our psyche or soul are formed by our immature thinking. It is of great significance for individuals to know and understand where their nature originated in order to comprehend the cause of immaturity. Both the nature of humanity with its immaturity and our higher nature can be reconciled.

David Hulse, D.D.

> *"For the creation (nature) was subjected to frailty—to futility, condemned to frustration—not because of some intentional fault on its part, but by the will of him who so subjected it {yet} with the hope."* (Romans 8:20, Amplified)

> *"Who hath saved us and called us with a holy calling, not according to our own works, but according to his own purpose and grace which was given us in Christ before the world began." (II Timothy 1:9).*

Each individual was given a nature before the foundation of the world. With that nature came a miraculous faculty for preservation in all situations. We were blamelessly subjected to frailty, futility, and condemned to frustration. However, this was for the precise purpose of bringing a higher design for the earth into full expression. Our individual nature, with its supposed weaknesses and evils, must be viewed through the light of a higher purpose, intention, and destiny. Life-long voids of frustration, anger, and total confusion will be filled through the understanding of our own unique nature.

Every one who continues the path of progressive truth will, at some point, think from the *nephesh* understanding: "I wish I could do it differently. I wish I could live my life over." Dealing with the conditions of life will continue to present great difficulty until one is able to say: "I would walk no differently. I would live my life no differently." You must embrace your nature and understand that it is from your own unique individuality that you learn, expand and prepare to teach and instruct others. **Intense hells are created out of a futile attempt to escape the very nature that was purposed and intended as a learning process.** (Hell can be described as an alienation from your true Self). This process unlocks a great ability, clothed in compassion, to relate to human fault and frailty.

Having not understood our immaturity, we often hide from others because of this lack of understanding. The true self is totally hidden, and the game of life is played by actors on a stage living their lives in an attempt to please others. Immaturity is a lack of expansion, a lack of growing up to the capacity or the element required for the full expression of each individual personality. In other words, we will continue to create and experience great voids of frustration, anger, confusion, lack and immaturity until we attain whatever element or capacity our own unique personalities require.

Voids are created during the first few years on the earth after the transition is made from spirit to matter. Limitations are set and accepted during the first few years of life from our infancy. During this period, decisions are made about how far in life one will go. These decisions are then reinforced through the adolescent years. By adulthood, patterns have been set, and we have programmed ourselves. With our own psychological script.

Throughout life, the conscious mind often makes decisions to break out of old patterns. However, if deep within sub-conscious programming, the ego does not believe it is possible, faithfulness to the set boundaries will soon be maintained at all cost. On rare occasions these boundaries and limitations may be exceeded, but soon the vows of faithfulness to the ego will be renewed. All actions will be counteracted and all outer manifestations will be brought back to the level of perception originally decided upon. It is we ourselves who will make sure that we do only what we have programmed ourselves to do. We will remain imprisoned within the boundaries the ego has set, condemning ourselves if we step out and move toward success and happiness. While we may deny this statement at the conscious level, the power to sabotage ourselves lies in the subconscious.

We may think we'd like to have a million dollars, meet the person of our dreams, or become successful in the business world; however, if our ego has accepted poverty, rejection, or failure, that is all we can experience. We will destroy anything that would take us away from the pattern that has been set.

A person with a strong mind may be able, for a season, to change the events of their outer world, yet remain in a state of total confusion within. Nothing they do will ever be enough because inner peace cannot be bought with material wealth or success. For this reason, the script cannot be rewritten through mental effort, or religious or emotional experiences. Only by contacting the Spirit of God—our higher self, *neshamah*, divine spirit-soul—can a new script be written! Hebrews 8:10 gives us a key to how this can be successfully accomplished.

> *"This is the covenant I will make with the house of Israel, AFTER THOSE DAYS, saith the Lord; I will put My laws into their MIND, and write them in their hearts, and I will be to them a God . . ."*

The word *after* expresses "association with that which is joined, participation, and accompaniment." Once the lower perception is aligned with our innate higher consciousness of knowing (remembering), we have then experienced the miracle – a shift in perception. Alignment can take place through techniques such as meditation, yoga, communing with nature and energy work.

"Positive thinking" alone has been ineffective because it does not address the cause of a situation. It may temporarily change an effect, but because the cause is not dealt with, it produces only false hope, which is only an illusionary feeling that will crumble all too soon because it is impossible to go beyond set boundaries. Clearing the mind to receive instructions from the Spirit, enables us to rewrite the script of life.

Two natures compete to survive—the nature of the divine spirit-soul, and the nature of the soul we have become through our own process of observing the world around us. *"The wolf (naphesh) shall dwell with the lamb (nameshah),"* Isaiah 11:6. Progression and maturity will harmonize these two natures into one beautiful melody. Experiences of the soul we have become, which was formed of our own free will, are the parts of our nature from which we learn true compassion. The divine spirit-soul breathed into the nostrils holds the original blueprint for a life free from disease, old age and death. With this blueprint comes a complete set of instructions how to build a body through which the higher self can express and manifest the reality of immortal life. How can we experience this shift in perception? The first step is to view all aspects of your life with great respect, no longer judging good or evil. Allow both facets of our nature to be transmuted and harmonized. This will bring amazing tranquility to our inner world. At this point, the shift in perception has begun! We are ready to embark upon a new phase of our journey into awakening and maturity. We will begin to receive instructions from our higher self that will set in motion a great readjustment to the events of the outer world.

UNDERSTANDING THE PSYCHOLOGICAL PROCESS

We have dealt with the importance of embracing our own unique nature. It is our own individual perception which makes up the part of our nature from which all challenges of life emerge. To accept and embrace all aspects of our nature, we must first have an understanding of certain elements which have been contributing factors in making our lives what they are.

It is necessary to begin at the inception of our entrance into the human realm, the moment of birth, to find an understanding of life beyond the surface level. During the first few months an infant does not know that it is separate from anything it sees around it. It has no perception of its own individual separateness. When it moves its hand, the whole world is moving. When its mother walks across the floor, the child perceives itself as walking across the floor. An infant is comfortable to remain at the mother's breast and be loved and fed, making no demands, for it is at ease in its oneness.

An awareness of total *at-one-ment* with everything is retained in the memory of the spirit as the experience of entering an infant mind and body begins. We were spirit without a body before we were clothed in a flesh body. As spirit beheld spirit, it could see no separation or division. We were spirit. Spirit was us. We had no idea or conception of a separate individual self-ego. This knowing remains with an infant for the first few months of its life.

Around the age of one to two, children begin to change. They are not as cuddly as they were during the first year or so of life. Suddenly, it is apparent they are no longer content to be held and confined. They become conscious of themselves as a separate entity. Interestingly, psychology defines this as the point where the child begins to experience his/her own individuality, the pseudo self (ego).

31

Facing individuality begins with the child's relationship to the mother. For example, she is not always there when the child wants a bottle or in the mood to play. She puts him in a playpen and allows him to cry, to let the child begin to realize it is separate from her. Not until the child is approaching adolescence does it actually begin to accept the fact of separation. According to psychological interpretation, although the child deals with its individuality through the years of one and two, the child is also holding on to the memory of at-one-ment with everything. The child believing it can retain it, is the reason the child becomes demanding and seemingly rebellious. In his new psyche that has begun to develop, the infant, it is still saying "You are one with me! You are me! Why aren't you there when I need you?" Eventually, the child accepts it is separate. They come into this earth void of any remembrance of separation, yet suddenly finds himself imprisoned in human flesh and form. A child literally goes through the shock of the human experience.

By the time the child has reached teenage years, they have forgotten their connection to Source and come to the belief that they are only a body. After careful consideration of all the facts that have been gathered thus far the child concludes, "I must conform if I am going to survive this human experience." At that point, they let go of the *at-one-ment* idea they had so desperately attempted to hold on to. They fall asleep to that in the world of matter, awakening to a new realization called the human consciousness, as a separate individual. The root of most psychological problems lies in the experiences encountered during this process. Usually this is the first years of life.

The transition from spirit to form has been easier for some than for others. Those who enter the earth realm with a higher spiritual purpose often encounter a different way of adapting to the human experience of separation. There was no one to help, for most of us, ease this transition because neither parents nor religion understood the process.

The principles we have dealt with thus far have not been taught in most religions. All too often people USE the Holy Spirit where others USE the bottle or drugs. The Holy Spirit was not given to be used as an escape from the reality of dealing with the problems and challenges of the world.

Problems cannot be solved just because we experience a spiritual high. The Holy Spirit teaches us how to face reality and deal with the issues of life.

This psychological process has affected us for thousands of years. The affects do not stop with the individual but are passed from one generation to the next. The axe must be laid to the root of the family tree! In most cases our parents' motives were sincere; however, we must realize they were not speaking from their hearts, but from programming that they received from their parents. There is great need for cellular restructuring of past as well as present generations. We can begin this cellular restructuring by learning to stop ourselves before we react to the words or deeds of another person. Step one is awareness; begin to evaluate the source of all feelings. Get in touch with our own emotions and stop worrying about the opinions of others. If someone does or says something that causes us to feel offense, or hurt, or causes certain thoughts to run through our mind, STOP and EXAMINE the source of the information that made us feel pain. When we take time to OBSERVE what made us perceive those words or actions as painful, we can trace back to the original root assumption.

We will be amazed at what we discover from our observation and examination. We will learn that many things we feel and say do not come from our true self. In the far recesses of our mind, a recording programmed by the opinions of parents, religion, culture, society, etc., begins to play. Both the opinions formed during the first few years of life and the inherited opinions recorded in the cells of the body speak through us as our opinions, prejudices, ideals, the way one looks at the world, viewpoints of God, of Jesus, beliefs of heaven and hell, etc. Our entire psychological makeup appears as our own individual feelings. Yet, in reality, few people are in contact with their true inner convictions.

We are continually fooled by emotions. Though lost and confused in the multitude of voices, the essence of the true self cries out: "Listen to me! Let me speak for myself!" That is called growing up. However, maturity is not acquired overnight. It develops and unfolds just as a rosebud blossoms into a beautiful rose when subjected to the proper elements of soil, water, light and time. One's journey into understanding the psychological process that has made man what he is must be embarked upon; however, this journey cannot begin until we become brave enough to birth our inner thoughts and convictions into our outer world. In other words, TO THINE OWN SELF BE TRUE! Individual growth and development demand direction and answers. Maturity will lead us on a search for truth, which cannot be found outside ourselves.

I once had a parakeet I dearly loved. Hudson could talk quite well, but I realized he did not know what he was actually saying, as he only mimicked and learned what he heard. Most times, it appears that people are no different. However, there is no inherent intelligence in *parroting*, or in being a carbon copy of other generations. They are just passing on the thoughts of others, rather than tapping into their own inner intelligence.

There is and will be more unique people on the earth who no longer allow the blind to lead the blind into a ditch of emotional human trauma void of guidance. People are beginning to speak out of their own truth. They are returning to what they knew in the beginning: that there is nothing separate from us. You are me, and I am you. God is us, and we are god. From this, a new generation is emerging. A genetically restructured people are beginning to walk this earth. The walls of division that have separated us from the reality of our true self will be surmounted. The spirit-soul that was breathed into our nostrils when we were created will be our guidance system.

THE MECHANICS OF MIRACLES

Earlier we made the statement that a miracle is a shift in perception. The word miracle in the King James text was taken from two different Greek words. One is *dunamis*, meaning, "power, strength, to be able or possible." The other is *semeion*, meaning "a mark, or indication." A miracle is a mark, or an indication of strength or power making something possible. These physical manifestations are considered miracles. In reality, however a miracle is the inner cause of the outer manifestation. In other words, a change in point of view enables one to comprehend or understand physical sensations. Simply put a shift in perception creates a miracle.

There is a point in spiritual growth where we are no longer content to seek only the outer effects of physical manifestations. A new force compels and initiates the aspiration to learn principles behind miracles. At this point, peace will be unattainable until the principles of miracles are uncovered and understood. We will no longer be content to pursue a god who just performs miracles. Personal experience becomes the school to learn the new principles.

That which has been called supernatural in the past era will become natural in the new era. Every time someone experiences any degree of physical manifestation in the form of healing or answered prayer, it is only a taste of that which is to come. Remember, consciousness objectifies itself as the outer conditions of our life. Many camp and pitch their tents short of the glory that is destined to be unveiled by settling for healing rather than health. They become part of a lesser glory and seek external miracles that can heal a disease, but leave the same inner condition that created the disease. The inner condition often creates another disease. Again healing is sought, and life becomes an endless cycle of sickness and healing. The cause of the sickness is never considered. There is a better way for us to live.

Some of those who settle for signs and wonders are unconcerned as to HOW a miracle takes place. We need to take time to understand the principle behind the miracle. To obtain the understanding which will enable us to do the "greater works" of which Jesus spoke.

When we finally cease from seeking external manifestations, we turn within to discover the inner workings of the higher self. For a time, we seemingly walk through a place of great void and emptiness, (Sometimes referred to as "the dark side of the Soul"). We are no longer able to find healing and deliverance outside of ourselves. We desire to learn the mechanics behind the principles that create the miracles. Those in preparation to be the educators of the new era will not find healing or miracles for many circumstances of life until they first understand the situations they desire to be freed from. They will no longer be content to seek healing or deliverance through outer religious rituals.

When an individual receives healing or deliverance, it sometimes only helps that individual. Other than perhaps sharing a testimony or building the faith of another, the healing or miracle is of no benefit in teaching humanity the principles behind the external manifestation. We, who have ears to hear, receive! Once we have a key to unlock the entire nature of creation, we will receive understanding of the situations from which we desire release. After we have fully experienced our present circumstances by walking through them, not running away or escaping from them, we will have answers for those who ask.

Thomas Edison tapped into a universal principle that has affected every civilization of this planet. It did not matter if those who knew him at the time of his intense research and experiments believed in him or not. It made no difference! The majority of people do not understand the mechanics of electricity, but they know how to flip a switch or insert a plug into an outlet. Edison uncovered a principle that is used by the entire world every day. It is not necessary to be taught the mechanics of electricity; yet, it is a part of life because someone took the time to unlock a principle that would be of great service to the entire world.

Understanding the principles behind miracles must begin with the individual. A shift in perception is only possible to us if we dare to face ourselves in complete honesty. Once we begin an examination of our self, through a higher discernment, only than can we begin to unlock the psychological patterns that have made us what we are today.

Honesty first begins by recognizing there is a child in each person that has never grown up and does not want to grow up. It will hide, cover and deny its childish ways by any possible means to escape the responsibility of facing its own immaturity. Honest examination could eradicate the need for drugs, alcohol or any stimulant that enables a person to lose touch with self. Addicts use artificial stimulants because they do not want to face that part of themselves that has never grown to maturity. They refuse to deal with the situations of life, hiding behind personality masquerades and artificial highs like little children who think that because they are under the covers the boogieman can't get them, or the storm can't hurt them.

The one who hides behind his religious emotional experiences is no different! This can become the very thing that causes us to escape what we need to face and deal with: our own psychological makeup, the adversary, or that which we DO NOT UNDERSTAND. A religious experience can literally abort the lessons we must learn to enable us to stop the endless cycles of repeated human trauma. All too often we are confined within the prison walls of defeat. Jesus gave specific instructions on how to stay out of prison:

". . . agree with your adversary quickly . . ." (Matt.5:25).

Agree comes from two Greek words meaning, "to be well-minded, mind, understanding." *Adversary* comes from a Greek word meaning "opponent," which Webster defines as "one that takes an opposite position, that which opposes (resists), or counteracts and limits actions." Therefore, to "agree with your adversary" means to mentally understand that which opposes, resists, counteracts and limits your actions. To understand is to "achieve a grasp of the nature, significance, or explanation of something." Know your adversary!

We have not understood the repeated patterns of the adversary which takes on multiple forms and disguises. We run from them, hide from them, or fight them—none of which brings understanding. Since the fourth century BCE, religion has declared; "Jesus is the only answer." We have been told that the way out of all trials and troubles is simply to repent and say, "Jesus, I'm sorry." We hide ourselves in the confines of the church and became another number, statistic in the masses, never again dealing with our negative patterns. The answer is not in a message about the man Jesus and the life He lived while on this earth. The answer is in the message He came to the earth to give. It is a message few have heard even after two thousand years of religious rhetoric. His message is one of how to deal with the adversaries of life through understanding the principles of miracles.

The majority of people have only known God for his acts, i.e. signs and wonders, but have never understood the process behind them. Religion has presented God as a miracle-worker far beyond human comprehension. As we grow spiritually, we will look at God from a different point of view. It is only when we come to this stage of development that we are able to find principles that will make life work. Life does not have to be a hit and miss thing of serving a God who will perform a miracle at one time in life, yet seemingly be totally deaf at other times. A shift in perception will give you the ability to ACHIEVE GENUINE MIRACLES that can change the tide of your life and turn defeat into victory! All who continue on the path of progressive truth will reach a place where the higher self will induce motivation to turn within to discover and unlock the principles contained in miracles.

Miracles or magic would best describe how external manifestations of signs and wonders are viewed by so-called "saints" and "sinners" throughout the ages. Each miracle Jesus performed carried within it a principle that, when understood and applied, enables us to experience the same benefits in our individual lives. I now want to look at two different accounts of Jesus feeding the five thousand as recorded in the Scriptures. Some would see them as a contradiction; however, if viewed from a metaphysical point of view, the two different accounts can be harmonized to teach a most profound principle that would raise mass consciousness. The miracle was not performed for the simple feat of satisfying five thousand hungry people on one particular day, nor was it performed only to meet the temporal needs of the moment.

I have taken the liberty to paraphrase the accounts of feeding the five thousand recorded in the King James Bible. In the first account, found in the fourteenth chapter of Matthew, we read that Jesus was moved with compassion for the multitude that followed Him. The disciples wanted to send the people away, but Jesus said: "They need not DEPART; give YE them to eat." In other words: *YOU give them something to eat, get involved with what I am doing. TOGETHER we can do something for the whole.* It was an invitation for collective participation in performing a miracle and teaching the principle behind the miracle.

The word "depart" means separation. Jesus was moved with compassion over the condition He saw in the people. Perhaps He was thinking: *They do not need to continue living their lives separated from what is essential to fulfill their needs.* The disciples' response was one of selfishness and unbelief. "WE have but five loaves and two fishes." In other words: *We only have enough for ourselves. If we give to the crowd there would be nothing left for us. Besides, how could this small portion of food feed so many?*

Jesus did not snap his fingers or wave a magic wand. He commanded the multitude to sit down. This is the first step in teaching the principles of a miracle. In other words, He was saying, "Sit down, relax, I am going to teach you something." Genuine miracles can be performed only when one is ready to receive instructions beyond his current belief system. Maturity declares, "No more instant magic!" In the sixth chapter of John we read another account. Jesus asked Philip, "Whence shall WE buy bread that these may eat?" Again, we see Jesus giving an invitation for the disciples' participation. Philip answered, "Two hundred penny worth of bread is not sufficient that each one might take a little." Philip represents the element in human nature that does not understand that a miracle can take place by collective participation using what is available and not by some super-natural power alone.

In this account, the lad is said to have the five loaves and two fishes. Andrew said to Jesus, *There is a lad with a little food, who wanted to give it, we thought he'd need it and besides, it could never feed all those people. So we didn't take what he had.* It is not the large portions that feed the multitudes, but each of us contributing whatever we have. The lad represents one who has the right motive and is not selfish or self-centered. He understands the principle behind a miracle. That the way to receive is to give. He willingly offered what he had. When the part of us that is in great need becomes weary with lack, we will turn to the higher self and receive what was once thought to be insufficient.

The lad had five loaves and two fishes, the same portion as the disciples. What was the difference in the lad and the disciples? The disciples were coming from self-centeredness. The lad was coming from a Christ-centeredness that said, "Here, take what I have." When he gave all he had, willingly and unselfishly, it moved through the entire group of people. Several in the crowd began to say, "Well, if that little lad can give his portion, then I'll give mine too." Someone else said, "I also only have a little. I didn't think it was enough to do any good, but here it is." As each individual willingly responded and gave what he had, it became enough to meet the need of the whole. This is how the entire multitude was fed. It did not fall out of the sky, but was accomplished through every person giving what he had, to finally become what was needed for the whole. If each one had looked at his portion individually, he would have thought it was not enough for the whole.

Jesus taught the principle of meeting the need by encouraging each of us to give whatever he or she has. The lad represents one who is living by one of the principles behind miracles. As one person after another begins to practice this principle, it will eventually tip the scales to the point of meeting the needs of all people. The disciples represent religious ministries that cannot hear what the Spirit is saying. Ministries have been built by performing miracles. When a person performs a miracle, then we rely on them for the next miracle. In the same way, a doctor who treats one part of our body becomes our family doctor because we know something will go wrong. We are actually preparing for another physical sickness. That's the reason some doctors are wealthy. That's why preachers who can perform so-called miracles are wealthy. People become dependent upon preachers for healing, deliverance and answers for each crisis they encounter.

The lad's need was also met when he unselfishly gave of his own substance to meet the need of the whole. Needs cannot be met by holding on to individual substance. Becoming part of a collective endeavor creates the miracle. This is spiritual growth! The world will turn its attention to those who are able to LIVE the principle behind miracles. Humanity will transcend lack and limitation by giving to receive with an attitude that says, "I will give to receive that I might receive to give." This is how individuals can become a channel to meet the needs of all, including themselves. However, it cannot work in an atmosphere of attitude that demands personal needs first. This principle teaches that as we give to meet the needs of the whole, our needs are met because we are a part of the whole.

What about the supernatural? In a small group of people, when every one participates with the portion he has, something beyond reason happens to meet the need supernaturally. Blessings come upon a group where ALL actively participate. This calls for individual responsibility and participation. It can become a reality much sooner when there is a genuine love and respect for each other. This is beautifully expressed by the words of the first governor of the Massachusetts Bay Colony, John Winthrop in 1630, "We must delight in each other, make others conditions our own, rejoice together, mourn together, labor and suffer together, always having before our eyes our community as members of the same body." Such an atmosphere as this would create miracles beyond mortal comprehension!

A willingness to experience all situations of life to the fullest will prepare us to receive and understand principles that will unlock the entire nature of creation. At this point, we are no longer satisfied to receive a supernatural miracle and be taken out of the challenges of life. This is where the shift in perception begins. By facing life head on, we will gain understanding of all situations that have opposed, resisted, and counteracted our actions. Genuine miracles will begin to take place in our lives. Individual willingness to share in collective participation to meet the needs of the whole will cause a chain reaction. Essentially, we must realize, there can be no collective participation without individual participation!

THIS IS OUR DESTINY

The psychological processes of the soul can appear as we allow ourselves to honestly examine the emotional patterns that control and manipulate our lives; however, we will find we do not think the same way we previously thought about a lot of things. Ideals and interpretations create great limitations that limit who we really are. When we allow our real SELVES to come forth, before we took on physical form, we see that same reality expressed in physical form.

There is no reason for another generation to project a lot of the nonsense on a future generation. As we take a stand in all affairs of our lives and declare that it is time for the tide to change, time for the wind to blow another direction, we can change the course of our lives.

God has stepped back and allowed us to rule this earth. All we have created can be recreated through a new pattern of thought. God has not interfered, but has permitted our free will to have control. The systems of this world, the kingdoms of this world—every dimension that our thoughts have ruled—can experience the reality of a higher power.

I have wonderful news! As the old belief systems that have been strengthened and reinforced from generation to generation grow weaker, there is another mind growing stronger. It is the awakening and standing up of the spirit-soul mind that was breathed into mankind many ages ago.

Divine expression will be communicated through the thoughts of this higher mind. As we listen for instructions and are quick to obey them, we will learn how to shorten the days of false hopes and illusions. Soon all the earth will be affected by the higher vibrations that echo from spirit through soul into physical form.

Collective consciousness is a layer in every person that retains a psychological memory of all thought that has ever been thought. Every thought is recorded in this layer. As Spirit taps into this layer, it will run through all levels of consciousness in everyone. It will travel as a vibration through the "face of the deep" (subconscious) and speak to the consciousness of all people, "Let there be light." The Genesis of life will begin in the consciousness of all creation: those now living in a physical body, those in the spiritual realm, and even those who occupy infant bodies. All thought will be permeated with pure light, as Spirit, expressed through the soul, travels and moves through the face of the deep, vibrating and fluttering into the consciousness of all.

We must expand into our inner depths to learn how to recreate the outer manifestations of life. It is time to transcend ego boundaries and leave the prisons of human weakness far behind in the memory of a soon-to-be-forgotten age of mortal limitation. Step out and love someone that religion, society, or culture said you couldn't love. Reach out and try a relationship where sex is not involved. Reach out and touch somebody without feeling lust in your heart. REACH OUT AND TOUCH SOMEBODY!! We need to experience having those of the opposite sex as friends without seducing them or using our charm to manipulate them. Reach out and touch people from a different level. Let love flow from the channel of our higher selves. Dare to experience life from a different point of view and begin the mortal assignment of transcending human limitations.

If you have children, be careful to discern them beyond their physical bodies. Know who they are, observe their actions, and listen to their words.

At this time there are many great spirit-beings incarnated in the bodies of the young. From time to time pure expression will flow through them as they are assisted in the transition from spirit into human experience.

Earth's inhabitants are about to be thrust into the greatest human transition of the ages. Humankind must be reunited with its destiny. The presence of love and harmony is enveloping this planet. The message of doom and destruction will soon lose its platform. The essence of life within each individual is longing to come forth. No one person can hinder nor prevent the magnitude of that which lies at the door of Planet Earth. Yet, each one is invited to participate in fulfilling the birth seen by the Apostle John over 1900 years ago: "Whosoever is born of God doth not commit sin; for His Seed remaineth in him: and HE CANNOT SIN, because HE IS BORN OF GOD" (I John 3:9). This is not a religious experience to be monopolized for profit. Rather it speaks of a new species who will no longer live in a sin consciousness. They will be born of God and incapable of sin for God's seed will remain in them. The promise made to Abraham many ages past will be fulfilled. A royal seed will fill this earth even in number as the stars of the heavens. A shift in perception will cause every fiber of our being to begin to respond to the vibrations of purpose and destiny intended for everyone walking the face of the earth! THIS IS OUR HERITAGE! THIS IS OUR DESTINY!

GOD ON ASSIGNMENT

IT IS NOT by accident that you have decided to read this book. You have been drawn to it, because at some time before you volunteered to come to this earth plane, you made a choice. The selection you made was to incarnate into your human form so you might play your part in the great plan of humanity's healing. The following illustration gives a picture of the choices you were given.

Two doors were offered:

Around the edges of one door beamed a radiance of pure white light, from which you could smell the fragrance of a flower-filled garden in the glory of spring.

You knew if you entered you would find the kingdom of heaven where there is total peace, love, everlasting joy, never ending abundance of all things, fullness of life and immortality.

Behind the other door was the absence of the white light due to ignorance, based on beliefs rooted in teachings of judgment and separation.

You knew selecting the door of light would allow you to retain who you truly are. It was the mournful cries for help coming from the other door that pierced your heart with compassion and love. We were drawn into that place where humanity had landed itself into the place of illusion and suffering. As it is written in *Psalms 7:15* "*They make a pit, digging it out, and fall into the hole that they have made.*"

By choosing an incarnation, and, because you said, "God, send me;

I will go," you have come to earth with an **assignment**. You are here as a light worker for humankind and that is why you find yourself walking through human conditions that are sometimes challenging. There is no way you would have chosen these experiences by your own desire or design after incarnating, therefore you would have had to have chosen prior to your incarnation. These experiences have been assigned to you so you will learn how to raise your consciousness and have more compassion for others in similar situations.

I want to encourage you not to fear any experience in which you might find yourself. If you are there by divine appointment, you will be protected in whatever you encounter. I found this quotation in an old book by Walter C. Lanyon that addresses the very subject on your protection on this mission:

"It all depends whether you are part of the Great Plan that is working out in this generation for the permanent ennoblement of mankind. If you are, then this is merely a means of your identification, showing you to be a person, not in life purely for experiences unto yourself but for the public good in the ultimate. If this is true, then you have your "pass" (as it were) through every type of danger. You should go forward with the confidence of the strong athlete or armored warrior, secure in the knowledge that a principle of Great Cosmic Physics is your shield and buckler, and that nothing can penetrate you." (*Out of the Clouds*, Bookhaven Press, Kellaway-Ide Co., Los Angeles, 1941, p.162).

As you are one who said, "I will go," your true identity can never be in danger, for you walk this earth as *GOD ON ASSIGNMENT.*

THE ESSENCE OF PURE RELIGION

Your day of separation is coming to an end! Some western religions teach you that your humanity is something evil, and therefore separate from God. Something that had to be *fixed* in order to be pleasing to God, ie: God is Spirit, but you are flesh.

This is the day that Spirit and flesh are coming together to form one new person. This is the end of humanity's religion and the beginning of pure religion.

The Bible speaks of religion just five times, but it refers to it only as PURE religion, e.g.,(James 1:26,27). The word *pure* in the Greek is translated as *transparent* or *clear*. Thinking about that, you may come to the understanding that your religion is not anything that should be seen. The only religion people should see is God in you. "Blessed are the pure in heart, for they shall see God." (*Matthew 5:8*) It doesn't mean the pure in heart shall see God, but rather, that *you are pure in heart, because you have already seen God as yourself and know who you are!* Therefore, when others look at you they shall see God in you, because all labels of humanity's religion will be gone. You will be transparent, having no trace of any religion of this world; your only desire being to manifest God.

Isaiah 45:14-15 says:

They shall come after thee; in chains they shall come over, and they shall fall down unto thee, they shall make supplication unto thee, saying, 'Surely God is in thee; and there is none else, there is no God. Verily, thou art a God that hidest thyself, O God of Israel, the Savior.'

This means they will find out God isn't who they thought God was, nor where they assumed God was! When they locate God, they will find God dwelling in people. The reason they can see God in you is because of your pure, transparent religion which means no religion at all.

God warned me the most difficult label for people to drop will be Christianity. That is because it is a man-made label. There is not an ounce of spiritual application in the term *Christian*. None whatsoever. The term, *Christian,* was first used by unenlightened people to label those who were followers of Christ. It was the people who were living in Antioch who first labeled the followers of Christ as *Christians.* They didn't call themselves *Christians*; they weren't inspired by the Spirit to call themselves that. It was a label put on them, and that label can keep people from seeing Christ in you. To attain pure religion, all the titles and labels will have to go. The term *Christianity* is fine when it refers to the experience of finding Christ

47

in you as the hope of glory, but don't keep it as a label because it tends to separate you from others beliefs.

God's intention is to appear and manifest in a pure, transparent people, free from any labels of religion. When they look at you, they won't see a label. They will see the divine.

GOD IN DISGUISE: THE MISSING PART

There is a aspect of God we are looking for that is not Spirit as religion has taught us. But there is a part of that Spirit disguised as human frailty and suffering. By finding ourselves in our humanity as spiritual beings we are bringing Spirit back into the Source of the Creator so we are being made whole in Spirit AND in human experience.

Because God is walking unrecognized in the earthly disguise of our humanity, God has not yet manifested as God in the flesh in this human realm.

I've been through many different experiences in my search for God. Even after going through many kinds of experiences, I still felt empty. I still felt like a part of me was missing. I still felt as though I had forgotten something. It was driving me crazy. What was it?

Then, God said, *"Me"*.

I said, "I thought I found You."

He said, "You forgot a part of Me that I gave to become your humanity. I am your humanity."

I'm not saying everyone's human experience is God. I am saying the masses of people who have fallen into the human experience are a part of the God Self which has taken on the form of fallen humanity. In that way, the flesh of the awakened one becomes aware of their deity.

As an offspring of God, you will not be whole until you embrace the deity of human experience. Love your human self, because it is part of God. Only then does the Creator and the Created become one. Get in touch with one another; reach out and start loving. You are God in human form. The coming together of God energy produces a God experience in human form.

Let your humanity be God's expression of itself in this world to redeem humankind, for this is the gathering of God's Self back unto source. God was made flesh, *Emmanuel*, and dwelt among us.

YOUR GOD FREQUENCY

You are God in disguise. Because you requested your assignment here on earth, your human experience carries a different frequency from the sea of humanity in this world. Even when we have tried to be a part of society we have felt that different frequency. You were there, but you weren't there. You will never be able to totally join with them, because God has taken you from among the things of the outer world to fulfill your inner purpose of soul. You are not the product of failure; you are not the product of sin. Your humanity is the product of God in the flesh. God is walking the earth in the guise of your humanity.

EMBRACING YOUR HUMANITY, STRUGGLING WITH HUMANITY

Because I have not really understood the purpose of my humanity until recently, I have spent many unenlightened years struggling with it, disliking it, and condemning it.

Religion taught me that God wanted me to be certain things in my humanity. That belief led me to the conclusion that my humanity was sinful and wrong. Since I sincerely desired to be pleasing to God, I tried numerous ways to conform my humanity to the perfection prescribed by the church. I spent many of my early years going around the country to deliverance ministries and engaged in a variety of practices in an attempt to conform into the image I believed God expected of me. I felt the need to save my humanity, redeem it and present it back to God.

I tried to overcome it. I tried to speak in tongues to change it. I tried to cast it out. I tried to fast it out. I tried to shout it out. I have been baptized in everybody's name you can think of, and some you can't even pronounce. I have taken communion every way you can name with everything you can take it with. I even went through a time when I felt the answer to communion was to use real wine—but only *Christian Brothers*. Anything else would have been worldly.

Now, I can sincerely tell you that none of this worked for me. I'm not saying it hasn't worked for others, but I can speak for myself when I say it did not accomplish the perfection in my flesh for which I had been striving.

Realizing none of these practices had changed my humanity. I sought to hide myself among a "spiritual" people so that I could live up to some illusion of what I thought I was supposed to be. I finally discovered the only way I could maintain this illusion was to stay away from people when I was not being the "anointed speaker". Only in the anointing could I be among people, for then my humanity was abated.

EMBRACING OURSELVES

Now I feel the day of hiding my humanity is over. Something has been fulfilled in me. I can somehow relate to Jesus two thousand years ago as He told those of His day that He had fulfilled the Law. He was saying He had tried and learned every aspect of the laws of His religion as the man Jesus. He had earned the position of Rabbi, a Master; He knew it all, and He could teach it. He had walked through everything and knew there was nowhere to go but to take a step into another dimension, to start a new age that would be known as the age of grace.

Having fulfilled everything about spirit as an invisible and intangible part of Self, I have awakened to realize it does not exclude my natural expression of walking through a human experience. Instead, Spirit enhances and embraces my humanity and brings it in. But I know I cannot be whole until I embrace all that I am in my humanity, as well as all that I am in my spiritual reality. I heard a voice say to me: "That which you are looking for does not go beyond your flesh but dwells within its substance. Quit running from it and walk through it. Live it! Taste it! Feel it! In it you shall find a great treasure!"

Let's be honest with ourselves. Would we have asked for some of the things we have had to walk through in our humanity? No! We would have asked for them only in our divinity. It was a *divine* request. We are in this world but we are not of it, and many of us are finding the reality of Spirit in our lives within the depths of our own humanity. We who have stopped running from our own human experience, have instead begun embracing it, finding a pearl of great price.

KNOWING OUR HUMANITY

We have come to the end of the day of "knowing no man after the flesh." Understand; We HAD to have that time of not judging one another, because we were too immature to understand the union of both the human and spiritual existence. We took our eyes off our humanity in one realm so we might return to understand it in another realm. This is one of those kingdom paradoxes we encounter from time to time. God takes something away in order to return it. We were taken away from the flesh only to be brought back to it in another realm of mature understanding.

When we are allowed to come back, we will return without judgment or condemnation. We will understand that the purpose of our journey through humanity is to merge our Spirit life with our human experience, so that we might become an inspiration to others held captive by similar human beliefs.

THE PURPOSE FOR OUR EXPERIENCE

This is a new age. The old world as we have known it has passed away. There is not just a new heaven but also a new earth; this is the healing of the separation of the Spirit and the natural into one Whole experience.

There has been a purpose to everything we have had to experience, both in our Spirit and our humanity. All this has been to mold us as an actual pattern—a coding of these experiences into our make-up so that we can impart them to others in the same way Jesus imparted the code of His human experiences to us. This pattern can be created only by the infusion of spirit into our humanity. It is a new day and a new way. Will we be made whole? This is not just a healing for one part of us. This is an integration that lifts all our experiences to the level of spirit and fuses everything together. No experiences have been in vain, even that we have called good and that we have called not good. Our humanity becomes God, as our experience is divine. Let's stop running from our humanity. Let's gather together everything we represent so nothing will be wasted. Let's embrace ALL we are in order to become a pattern for Christ, as Jesus was.

SON OR DAUGHTER OF GOD AND HUMANITY
THE UNIVERSAL CONNECTION

As I began to re-evaluate my human experience as an integral part of my assignment as a pattern for Christ, I realized I had to address the question of sin. I had been interpreting my humanity as something sinful, something evil. If I had been, assigned here to walk through certain experiences for the benefit of others, then I had to have a new understanding to accomplish my assignment.

My search brought me to a statement in a book called *A Course in Miracles* that completely revolutionized my concept of sin and of who I am. In it Jesus said, "Forgive me all the sins you think the Son of God committed. And in the light of your forgiveness he will remember who he is, and forget what never was. I ask for your forgiveness, for if you are guilty, so must I be"

Reading those words touched me, and gave me a whole new viewpoint of myself. If I declared myself a sinner, then I had to call Jesus a sinner as we share the Sonship. What a major shift in perception that was!

IDENTITY AS A SAVIOR

Suddenly I had to know WHY I had been taught Jesus was the Savior of the world. The first thing that came to mind was His virgin birth. I know there are a lot of mixed opinions about the virgin birth as a historical event, but I understood the historical birth through the Virgin Mary as a reflection of the Christ being born through the virgin womb of consciousness, I'm using the term virgin to mean that part of the higher consciousness that is yet to be penetrated by outside society, culture or religion. Remember they tell us we only use approximately 10% of our consciousness. Knowledge will just pour out of the 90% of untapped, not penetrated, part of the mind where the womb has been shut until this day of overshadowing by the Most High. His being born from the virgin mind. Then what is true of The Christ is also true of me. And what is true of me is true of YOU!

Our true mother is our virgin mind. When we start to believe and appropriate that, truth will begin flowing from us which has never thought before. Some things will be formed in us that are not going to be *about* the Spirit but are going to BE the Spirit expressing itself. Remembering the Bible states that Jesus said "my words are Spirit," I then understood that Jesus knew He wasn't a sinner because He realized His true origin. He recognized He had come from the incorruptible seed of the virgin mother and Most High God/Father. He knew "Whoever is born of God doth not commit sin; for his seed remaineth in him: and he cannot sin, because he is born of God." (*1 John 3:9*).

BEING MADE SIN

However, the Bible says that Jesus was MADE sin. There is a difference between a person who is a sinner and a person who is made sin. That means you can be made sin, and yet, not be a sinner. Jesus was made sin so that He could help humanity. He could not accomplish that by simply remaining the Divine Son of God, but also becoming the Son of Man.

Leviticus 16 gives instructions concerning the ritual of atonement whereby, two goats were made to be sin. The high priest cast lots for these two goats in order to determine which goat would be sacrificed as a sin offering and which goat would remain alive to carry all the sins of Israel into the wilderness.

Note that these animals were chosen by lot. Like them, we did not pick and choose some of the things we have had to bear in this life, (or did we); or were they assigned to us by lot (fate)?

By having have hands laid on them, both goats had the sins imparted to them. Each carried within its flesh all sins of the people of Israel, for one full year. The goat carried no sin of its own, but was made sin by the sins of the people being imparted to the flesh of the goat. OUR humanity IS God made sin, but OUR experience is divine.

The sacrifice of the first goat was tremendously important in this plan, not only because of its role concerning the iniquities of the people, but also because of what its death meant to the second goat. The sacrifice of the first gave life to the second. The place of the second goat in this great program of atonement was its LIFE. It was kept alive, and the effect it would have on the iniquities of the people was evidenced in the fact that it lived. The goat that remained alive was called the scapegoat, and that is the part we play.

DRIVEN BY A FIT PERSON

This scapegoat was very important and unique because it was driven to its destiny by the people in its life. Leviticus 16:21, *22* states the scapegoat was driven into the wilderness *by the hand of a FIT man*. The word "fit" in the Hebrew in *Strong's Concordance* means "timely." *A fit man* is a timely person in our lives who is used by Spirit to drive us to a certain place where we may experience a particular part of human experience.

The best *Bible* example I can give of a fit man is Pharoah. For 430 years, the children of Israel talked about leaving Egypt to enter into the land Yahweh had promised them. But all they ever did was TALK about leaving the land of Egypt, until Yahweh raised up Pharaoh, and hardened his heart in order to drive Israel out of their complacency, and eventually bring them to the land that was promised to them.

THE TRUTH SHALL MAKE US FREE

We can totally free ourselves and anyone else in our lives whom we feel has treated us wrongly only if we understand *the principle of the fit man*. We have walked a unique path through our human experience in this world, driven by people whose hearts God has hardened toward us. I am convinced there are some people in my own life who have mistreated me who would not have chosen to do so. Rather, God used them to cause me to move me on my path toward destiny. Now I can pray for my enemies and love those who have persecuted me, because I realize they have all been timely people directing me to walk through an experience that caused me to stand up and declare the appearance of God in humanity. This is not the appearing of God in spirit, but the appearing in HUMANITY.

OUR MISTAKE IN IDENTITY

Having been sent here as a part of God, we took on a human identity which we equated with being a sinner. We have been under the false belief that some religious experience would deliver us from our sinful state. I have found this not be true. When we come here, we bring our Godhood with us. It is our true seed identity. We do not get our true identity from man made religions, as we bring it with us when we incarnate. Some of us may have felt more different from others and as though we didn't always fit in. Because of our need of acceptance from others we chose to identify with our human self forgetting our divine self. This is why it is important for the Holy Spirit to bring back our true identity to remembrance.

THE HUMANITY OF THE CHOSEN

I have been a little uncomfortable with using the word *chosen* the way it has been promoted. The implication we get when we allow the ego to influence the definition of the word *chosen* is that we are special, separate, and exclusive. When we pass the idea of being chosen through the Holy Spirit, it takes on a new meaning and brings unity as opposed to separation. It will draw us to everything. By the Holy Spirit's definition, being chosen will draw us to walk among everything without being exclusive from anything.

A person who is chosen is one who chooses what God has chosen. God has only one Son, and He is THE Chosen. That means the Seed of God in every person is chosen; however, not every person has chosen the will of God. Although Jesus had chosen God's will and was the chosen of

God, when it came to His tribulation in the garden, He still had to align His will to God's.

I use the term *chosen* to mean that by choosing what God has chosen. We become *the chosen*. (*"If any two agree on earth as touching anything, it shall be done." Matt. 18:19*)

I see a people rising out of religion to become a city set on a hill, the Zion of the Lord. Yet, at the same time, I am still connected to everyone I don't see in that company, because I know the divine seed dwells in those asleep in the prison of humanity, just as surely as it abides in us who have chosen God's path. Because I am the chosen, I can unite with them; yet I can take my place in the plan God is bringing forth in the earth.

There are a *people* on the earth today who have infused their human experience with their spirit. There is a *people* who know they are the called and have chosen to follow that calling. There is a *people* who understand their humanity is not at enmity with God; a *people* who identify themselves as the Sons and Daughters of God and the Sons and Daughters of Humanity.

SALVATION UNTO GOD: MISSING THE CHARACTER

The chief problem of humanity is that we have lost contact with our original identity. When we are not centered in knowing who we really are, we live in a separate state of consciousness. This separate state of mind is known as a sin consciousness.

The definition of the Greek word *sin* in Strong's *Concordance* literally means "to miss the mark". It is an archery term used when someone misses the bull's eye. It means "not centered". Every time our mind is not centered in who we really are, we are in a sin consciousness, which means we have missed the mark.

The word *mark* comes from the Greek word *charagma*. It is the root from which the English word "character" comes. So, to sin really means to miss our true character or nature.

THE LOWERING OF THE CREATOR

We know our true Father is the Father of spirits. If God is spirit, then the Offspring is spirit also. If that is true, then what has fallen into lower frequencies to take us on what we call the human experience? God didn't create human beings in heaven who mess up and were cast down to earth to be labeled sinners. Before there was anything, there was nothing except the very void of Life itself. Life couldn't produce anything but life. The Creator and the created were one. How can they be separated? Nothing can separate us from the love of God – not angels, not dominions, not powers, not devils, not demons, not sin. NOTHING CAN SEPARATE US FROM THE LOVE OF GOD. We are eternally secure within the creative aspect of our expression and being. Religion tells us, "we did something to separate us from our source". At that point the creator became angry at his own creation which he threw out of heaven and we became sinners—fallen mutated beings so vastly unlike the Creator that we are now unrecognizable as divine beings.

UNDERSTANDING THE SON OR DAUGHTER

I don't see it that way any more because, the story of the prodigal son from Luke the 15th chapter, which gave me a new understanding. Influenced by an oriental proverb, the story of the prodigal, that had originated thousands of years before the Bible. This ancient proverb indicated because God was the only one in the universe, became a little bored, and said, "I think I'll lose a part of Myself and see if it can find its way back home."

I had an epiphany and I knew there was something to this idea. I then understood that the story of the prodigal son was an interpretation of the duality of human thinking. A split mind saw one son with two different perceptions.

There is the Son who never goes anywhere, who remains with the Father and cannot be separated. Then there is the perception of the son who leaves his Father's house and goes into riotous living, spends all his money and ends up in the swine pen. When our duality is healed and our eye becomes single, we can see it is the same son.

The created Son or Daughter never went anywhere. They can't go anywhere, because they are what God is—a state of Being. The story of the son or daughter who went to the swine pen is the perception of what was going on in the mind of the son and daughter who didn't go anywhere. Remember ideas can never leave there source. It's was a dream, an illusion, what eastern philosophy calls Maya. The MIND of the created Son or Daughter wasn't where they perceived themselves to be.

When we awaken, we will discover that we are that part of God that has never gone anywhere. We will find we are the created Son or Daughter *having* the dream. We are that part of God that changes not. We didn't change into the Son or Daughter in the swine pen. You have always been the sinless, guiltless created Son or Daughter of God.

The Son or Daughter in the swine pen is what the separate mind made when we believed we lost a part of ourselves and need to find our way back. Now, we are beginning to awaken to the part of us that has never gone anywhere. As we always remain the divine idea in the universal mind of the creator.

HOLY GROUND

Humanity is God who has been separated in thinking but not in being. God took out of Himself and reproduced Himself in like-kind called Holy Ground. The most Holy Ground we can meet on is the ground of existence—the I AM. When we become this Holy Ground, it doesn't matter if we are male or female, bond or free, Jew or Gentile, or whether we believe in heaven or hell, because we are all part of the same Source. We are all in the I AM, because simply, we exist.

When we discover God in us as ourselves, we find the Existing One. That is the ONE BEFORE the ONE spoken of in GENESIS. Genesis didn't start out with the Existing One; it started out with the Elohim, a plural expression. The God behind the Elohim, is the I AM, the Existing

One. This is the true Father and Mother, the starter and nurturer of all things.

OUR MIS-CREATION

We were a part of the deity that originally began to create, but due to separate ego based thinking, we ended up mis-creating (forming what had been created). As divine beings we left our Source behind and tried to become like the Creator, and thereby parented a mis-creation, resulting in the situation that we now have. In other words, we are responsible for this condition.

RAISING OUR DIVINITY

If there was indeed part of God who ended up into this mis-creation, then there must also be that part that needs to be saved and brought back into Oneness. This seems incredible. God needs to be saved? Could this be true? Then, a scripture was given to me that confirmed my thought; *"SALVATION' UNTO OUR GOD AND UNTO THE LAMB THAT SITTETH UPON THE THRONE." (Revelation 7:10).* Salvation unto GOD? I was looking for MY salvation! Then the Spirit said, "Didn't you just get up last night and preach that your own true self IS God?" What needs to be redeemed? What needs to be brought back? It is SPIRIT! SPIRIT returns back to God who gave it. God so loved the world that God gave Itself which is you. God gave YOU! SALVATION IS UNTO GOD IN HUMAN EXPERIENCE!

ACCEPTING OUR ASSIGNMENT THE UNLIKELY PATH

In order to raise up the part of God entangled in the mis-creation of humanity, some of us have been asked to walk a path that seems totally foreign to the world of Christianity because it looks like the way of flesh. However our designation is not a license to do what is not in alignment with our higher purpose. It is, however, an assignment appointed to us, and we will do what we HAVE to do. It appears there is no free choice, but the

59

truth is we have already chosen our contracts previous to our incarnation. Therefore it is written in our soul script and encoded in our cells of our body to be activated at the appropriate time.

Some of us feel trapped, inexplicably trapped in human weaknesses from which we have tried again and again to free ourselves, failing to do so. The very reason we have not been able to deliver our base humanity is because we can't get rid of that which is God in our human experience. Whatever is genetically passed through the natural blood line, can be dissipated, freed and released; but whatever is *"God on assignment"* will remain.

We have probably had people repeatedly warn us to stop our "errant" behavior, telling us what a mess this thing was going to be, but we felt absolutely helpless to get away from the situation. All their advice accomplished was to make us rebellious and more stubborn, a rebel, unruly to parents, religion and churches. It is not that we wanted to be in that situation. We would have given anything to be free of that human frailty, but we sensed we HAD to be in that experience.

It is no different for us than it was for Paul. He felt he needed to have certain improvements in his flesh to become more effective with the Word and the revelation God was bringing forth through him. He also struggled with what he called *a thorn in his flesh.* He prayed and asked God to change it. "Please deliver me!" But God said nothing. He prayed again and again. God did not answer. Paul prayed a third time concerning the matter, he received no response from God. Finally, when the answer came, it was not at all what Paul expected. He thought the answer would be some kind of tremendous physical change. It wasn't. Instead, it was just a word deep down inside him, and the word said, "Cool it. Don't waste your energy, for I have caused this thorn in your flesh. I caused this messenger to come. See Me in this, Paul. My grace is sufficient for thee."

And, if we are being true to ourselves, we know we too, have had to walk in particular circumstances, because we, too, are *"God on assignment"*.

IN THE LIKENESS OF SINFUL FLESH

Some of us may have experienced what we would call "hell" in our life; however, we do not experience this type of suffering for our benefit only, but for the benefit of others caught in activity of similar situations. Some may have to walk into the jaws of death, to remove the sting of death.

Others may have to walk through such human experiences as drugs, alcohol etc. Those in Alcoholics Anonymous are there to break the power of the problem when they understand their own divinity as *"God on assignment"*. Even though they may not want to find themselves in this situation, at a deep level they know they are there to free others in the same situation, they are *"God on assignment"*.

IN ALL REALMS OF HUMANITY

God is injecting substance into every walk of life in order to raise it to a higher plane. I want to encourage those who have not been successful in relationships in the past to know that you can have a relationship where *"God is on assignment"*. These are the only relationships that will work.

The institution of marriage as we know it has not worked because we have not been joined with others who are also sharing this assignment to raise the frequency of human experience. Relationships in the kingdom will not isolate two people, for there can be no jealousy, insecurity, or self-possession in this era we are entering. As we have awakened to knowing we are *"God on assignment"* we will be free of self-guilt.

"God is on assignment" all over the planet. You who are drawn to read this are *"God on Assignment"* in your city & state. God is living out the human experience, but some do not recognize God in the disguise of human experience. They did not know God 2000 years ago in the form chosen then; so don't be surprised if they do not recognize God in/as you.

There have been those confined within religion that have misunderstood and therefore judged us. I have heard in some cases

61

about those who have been thrown out of their own churches. We should all be discerning about who we judge for the bible tell us we should not "touch gods anointed".

For 2000 years, religion has been unable to keep us from remembering who we truly are as gods. (*John 10:34, Psalms 82:6*) Who God truly is shall soon be revealed as we enter this time of the awakening of consciousness, for we have been in this dream long enough, and this is the time to awake. I believe that where the bible tells us that there are "multitudes and multitudes in the valley of decision" there are many ready to follow the path toward Self-realization. They will know God and see God appearing among the human experience as they did with Jesus.

RECEIVING OUR TOTALITY

You cannot run from your assignment. If there were anywhere to run, I would already be on my way. Wouldn't you? Let me save you the trouble. Stop looking for a place to go, somewhere to hide. For out of our humanity will come the Song of the Lord that no one can learn until it is given by the inner voice of reality.

God has been imprisoned in our humanity long enough. That's why it is written. Jesus "preached to the spirits in prison". It does not say what he ministered to them about, but I'm going to take the liberty here to believe he told them of the day (this day) that the Divine would be free from the ignorance of human experience.

However, this is the acceptable year. This is the Day of **our** salvation. It is time to set the prisoner free. God needs to be recognized, called out and released in our humanity to become *"God on Assignment"*. **The prisoner is not our humanity; our prisoner is God!** God has been imprisoned in our humanity, but we are getting ready to see God be set free IN our human experience; this is the coming of the Lord. *1 John 2:28*

The spirit returns to God who gave it. When our flesh is returned to the Spirit, we will know we are connected to the Source, for our humanity will be vibrating at a new frequency—the Frequency of Life.

By releasing God in us we become whole. Being made whole in our flesh IS *"God on Assignment"*. Let's make a decision to be whole, to be all that we really are. Let's relinquish judgment and condemnation on any part of our human self. Let's embrace everything we are; for in so doing, we will stand on this earth as *"GOD ON ASSIGNMENT"*.

COMING IN YOUR OWN NAME

THE ORDER OF LIFE

In the beginning, when God the Father extended Himself into creation, by virtue of God's nature, an order or hierarchy of life established, so that the universe would interact in love and harmony. Honoring this order of things came naturally to us in our original state, because we were aware of God in all creation.

Something happened in our minds, however, and we began to think of ourselves as something other than the exquisite Divine Being we were created to be. We became a weakened, "hued-down" person, a hu-man. Losing the memory of our original identity threw the entire planet into disorder and disharmony.

Everything we have been experiencing is designed to restore us to proper order. When divine order is re-established within us, we will automatically honor life as part of our true nature.

INTENDED ORDER

THE HUMAN BEING

ANTHROPO IS A prefix that means *a* "human being". *Anthropocentric* is a word that means "regarding humans as the universe's most centered entity". The divine order of hierarchy was to begin with the man-kind, the God-Self, the person we were created to be. Man-kind was to be at the top of the order, because humans were given partnership over the Earth. Recognizing our true identity we will function in this position of co-creative partnership.

THE ANGELIC ORDER

The angelic order was created to serve with mankind by assisting us upon the planet. When mankind would need assistance, they called on the spiritual beings in the angelic realm to help them.

However, when mankind became a more diluted version called the *hu-man,* we lost our connection with our own angelic nature. At that time the order of things changed and we moved into the order of separation.

We are just beginning to remember who we truly are; we are the angels we are looking for. Some of us as angelic beings chose to incarnate into the human experience, while others chose to stay in the spirit realm.

The word *angel* as translated from the Greek in to English actually means "messenger." These spiritual angels appear to us in the form of inner intuitive guidance. With this is the type of inner guidance we will see our reality align with our souls path.

THE ANIMAL KINGDOM

Next in the order of creation was the animal kingdom. The only difference between the human kingdom and the animal kingdom is the evolutionary development of the frontal cortex with its ability to act on free-will & imagination. Animals have a consciousness, and they incarnate, just as other life forms incarnate, from the overall pre-physical soul of the planet.

This kingdom must be totally re-evaluated, because a lot of what is wrong with the planet right now is the fact that things are not in divine order concerning animals. Animals were given into the care of humans. Humans were to have a loving partnership (not a cruel, destructive, tyrannous control) over all animal and plant life.

Animals were not given to us to slaughter for our food. Most of the meat we buy in our grocery stores and other places is slaughtered meat. It has been proven that slaughtered meat contains chemicals that are produced from the fear, trauma, stress, and confusion the animal experiences, during the unspeakably cruel slaughtering process. By eating this meat, we ingest chemicals produced from the fear and anxiety the animal has suffered. Furthermore, this meat also contains antibiotics, hormones, and all types of artificial substances given to the animal for the purpose of enhancing its weight and physical development. And we wonder why, it is difficult for some us to control our weight! One alternative is to purchase organically raised meat that doesn't contain artificial chemicals. The best thing is to enter a state of consciousness where meat is not desired.

If you notice in the natural balance of things, a hunted animal, stalked by another animal for prey, during the process of the chase, the hunted animal drops, and its eyes become glassy as it gives itself up to the perusing animal. Because the soul of the hunted animal departs the body before it is ever eaten, the animal never experiences the pain of being eaten. In other words, an animal will give itself up through a natural law that eliminates the pain, the stress, and the suffering that other animals experience during slaughter. Nature's way is in divine order, while the savage cruelty of humanity is far from it.

I'm not trying to convert us to eating vegetables as a discipline, but rather encouraging us that by embracing our true nature as Sons and Daughters of God, we will naturally loose all taste and no desire for slaughtered meat, as we move into our true place in divine order.

THE CALL TO RETURN

Earth is a dysfunctional planet because we are not working with the Spiritual Laws of the Universe that make us free from ignorance (sin) and death. Once we come into harmony with this universal law, struggle is eliminated and we have life more abundantly.

One of the reasons we are so stressed out is that we have to work hard for happiness. We have to work hard for love. It's not naturally easy for people to fall in love, and get along and live in harmony. We have to work hard at it. We get stressed out trying to keep our marriages together and trying to keep our families together. Maybe, we should ask, "If it takes this much effort, is there a better way?" Yes. There is a better quality of life. It comes from returning to your divine identity and finding place in our divine order.

OUR RESPONSIBILITY

Returning to our Divine Self is not optional. We have a responsibility to come into our own divine order. Responsibility is simply the ability to respond to the leadership of our innate spirit. When we do that, we will help change the course of our world.

Standing up and responding in accordance with our divine order and identity is the very subject addressed in *Psalm 82.*

1. *God standeth in the congregation of the mighty;*
   He judgeth among the gods.
2. *How long will ye judge unjustly,*
   and accept the persons of the wicked?
3. *Defend the poor and fatherless,*
   do justice to the afflicted and needy.
4. *Deliver the poor and needy,*
   rid them out of the hand of the wicked.
5. *They know not, neither will they understand;*

> *they walk on in darkness, all the foundations*
> *of the earth are out of course.*
> 6. *I have said, Ye are gods,*
>   *and all of you are children of the Most High.*
> 7. *But ye shall die like men,*
>   *and fall like one of the princes.*
> 8. *Arise, O God, judge the earth,*
>   *for thou shalt inherit all nations.*

God standeth in the congregation of the mighty; He judgeth among the gods.

This judging is God restoring order. Order attracts everything we need into our lives. We don't have to be desperate anymore. We don't have to run out and get married because we're desperate or lonely. Something is wrong if desperation is the motivating factor behind our actions and our choices. Our choices can be spontaneously right actions, not involuntary spasms forced by desperation. We can move and respond every minute of our lives without analyzing our actions; we can move in harmony with the flow of our life force energy. We can spontaneously attract everything we need into our lives to give us the best possible quality of life. If not, we may be living outside our divine order.

How long will ye judge unjustly, and accept the persons of the wicked ? (*Psalm 82:2*)

In other words, when we judge people as wicked, they are wicked only because of our perceptions of them. No one is wicked; only our perception of them is wicked. We can stop trying to change people we think are wicked by changing the way we think about them.

Religion teaches us to save everybody by forcing them to think as we do which sometimes gives us happiness. Ironically, this causes most of the unhappiness in the world. People are angry because they can't control and manipulate everyone else to be what they want them to be. We secretly think, "How can I be happy until I can get everybody else to live life the way I think is right?" Mostly it is our own perceptions that need to be saved and healed.

> *Defend the poor and fatherless,*
> *do justice to the afflicted and needy.*
> *Deliver the poor and needy,*
> *rid them out of the hand of the wicked. (Psalm 82:3-4)*

God is saying, "How long are you going to misuse your creative powers to manipulate and control? When are you going to stop and trust the process?"

Fear prevents us from trusting this wonderful natural River of Life, this beautiful flow of energy that is available to us. We disrupt the natural flow with vain attempts to fix our own problems.

By coming into divine order, we see no need to manipulate because Spirit itself will heal and correct. We find that waiting in an attitude of pure love develops trust and faith, to take people where they need be.

> *They know not, neither will they understand;*
> *they walk on in darkness; all the foundations*
> *of the earth are out of course. I have said,*
> *Ye are gods, and all of you are children*
> *of the Most High. But ye shall die like men,*
> *and fall like one of the princes. (Psalm 82:5-7)*

I hear the Creator saying, "You are all My children. You all are co-creators. You all are created in My image and likeness, which is love. You are all children of the light. You are all Spirit.

But . . . You shall die like men. You are not going to live like God. You are going to die like men—*humans*, and fall like one of the princes (of this world).

It is all because you have not found your true identity within yourselves. Have I not said, 'Ye are gods, children who bear My very name'?

Arise, O God, judge the earth, for thou shalt inherit all nations.
(Psalm 82:8)

We are the God-Beings being called to arise. Let's judge the earth righteously. Let us see no evil, no sin, no condemnation. Let us see Christ in each face. Let us see

each one as a divine brother or sister. In this righteous judgment, we will receive our inheritance.

Notice, however, your reward is not streets of gold and a mansion in heaven. We're not going to build our mansions next door to Jesus. No, we will inherit the nations, the heathen. What we will inherit has nothing to do with streets of gold and pie in the sky; we've inherited the problems of this planet. The very thing we would like to run from is what we are going to inherit. The pain, the suffering, the groaning of humanity is our inheritance.

It is only the full grown Sons and Daughters who are able to receive this inheritance, due to their maturity of their spiritual understanding of divine order.

THE NAME OF GOD

God's name is a universal family name of which we are a part. We share the same name with God, because the whole family in heaven and earth has been given that name. The name of the basic, essential and intrinsic nature of all creation is . . . . . I AM.

TRADITIONAL CHURCH VIEW

Ironically, traditional Christianity is not built upon the premise of the universal family name "I AM", but rather, upon the premise of the individual name "Jesus."

The fact we have believed the foundational name of Christianity is Jesus gives validation to the idea of separation. My name is not Jesus and probably, neither is yours. (Unless you're from Hispanic decent) Jesus is a very unique but individual person.

When I say "Man", I am not talking about a gender; I am referring to the species of mankind, a human being (Greek, *anthropo*). Human beings are about spirit (breath) or divinity manifesting themselves all the way to cellular appearance. Few have made that kind of manifestation on this planet.

Jesus was that kind of Man, however. Two thousand years ago, humans looked at Him and said, "What manner of Man is this?" They knew there was something different about Jesus. Jesus did not come short of the glory. Not many Men or Women who have lived on this planet have attained union of spirit and body manifested as one.

Being so busy learning who Jesus is has kept us from perceiving that *who Jesus is* should bring us back to *who we are*. Masses of people in fundamentalist churches recognize Jesus as the only Son of God, but they don't believe they are, too. When you really know Jesus is the Son of God, you'll understand you are a part of the Sonship.

UNDERSTANDING THE NAME

In places where the Bible says, "Be baptized in My Name," or "Whatever you ask in My Name," the church teaches that name refers to Jesus. When you hear, "I am the Way; I am the Truth; I am the Life," you may think those words came **from** Jesus, they did not. Those words came **through** Jesus from a deeper premise of identity within. Jesus was speaking as a mediator of the I AM presence.

THE ESSENCE OF THE NAME

Jesus said, *"I go to prepare a place for you that where I am, you may be also."* The place Jesus was referring to was the place I AM. That is Jesus' real name. Every time He said do this or ask this in my name, He wasn't telling us to use the name Jesus, but the name I AM, which comes from that place within ourselves.

This is why life worked for Jesus, and why life often doesn't always work for us. Jesus stayed true to his true name, *I AM*. He didn't go around with labels put on him by society but remained true to his own essence.

INSIDE THE FAMILY

The name *"I AM"* doesn't belong to only one person. Every individual person that has lived has begun from the most sacred point in consciousness by stating *"I AM"*, whether it would be *"I AM"* a Christian, *"I AM"* an Alcoholic, *"I AM"* a Republican or Democrat or even *"I AM"* an Atheist. Even before any of these labels were stated they all had to begin from the statement *"I AM"*. The one absolute truth we all share is the truth of existence itself. El, one of the meanings of God, means the existing one. If the human ego can get us to project onto something separate from ourselves, it leaves us outside the "family".

Certain rights accompany family intimacy. For example, I may invite you to my house and say to you that you can have anything you want that's in my refrigerator, but most likely, you will not really feel comfortable enough to do that. However, when you go to your family's house, there is a different intimacy; you will feel free to exercise liberties you would not take with anybody else, even though they may have been offered to you.

Likewise, if you keep other people's children one of the parents may say, "I give you permission to correct my child or do whatever you see fit." I guarantee that because it is not your child you'll be a little more careful, no matter how much freedom the parent has given you. You won't take the same kind of liberty as you would with your own child.

Being in the family allows us to share the same spiritual name in order to enjoy all the intimacies and the blessings of family life. Most importantly it's not the separate name *"Jesus"*, but the universal, spiritual family name of the *"I AM"* where we live and move and have are being.

This is why we must give reverence and honor to each other, regardless how much we might disagree with the way others define their living, no matter how much we disagree with their actions or the choices they make in their lives. We must honor the fact that each person is a unique

David Hulse, D.D.

expression of life, a member of the same family who shares the same name with us.

THE POWER OF THOUGHT—OUR NAME CODE

Every part of creation not only has an individual soul, but also, is part of a collective planetary soul. If we think, live and breathe, regardless whether we are a homeless person on the street or a rich socialite living in a mansion, we contribute to the overall soul of the planet.

As a Son or Daughter of God, we are undeniably powerful because every thought that we qualify as a reality by our belief system is coded with our unique "*I AM*" name. Therefore we must ask ourselves, "Does this thought, when deposited into the collective consciousness, lift and edify all, or does it perpetuate the lies of limitation? "*I AM*" is universal—One—but, because of this individual code, there is no single one who is the same "*I AM*" that we are in universalism. The uniqueness of the "*I AM*" expression is that we are on the planet. In other words, we are united as one in the universal, but we are each the individualization of that one. We all have our own path to remembrance.

THE POWER OF CHOICE

Will is powerful, because it compromises an element of creativity. Even if we choose unwisely, our intention carries the same power to create as it does when we choose wisely. In other words, we can use our will to murder, which manifests and creates death; or, we can save somebody to manifest life. The same power runs through whichever choice we make – wise or unwise – because divine power creates without distinction. This is why we have a world of what we perceive to be both good and evil. The power that creates good and evil is a neutral power that of itself it is neither good nor evil. God just is. Consequently, we must take responsibility for what we create as our reality, because whatever we believe to be real is a seed – thought that produces after its own kind.

God moves through our choices, our imagination and our thinking processes. Whatever we choose and qualify by, and saying what we believe, is marked by our individualized code name *I AM*. Furthermore, whatever we choose not only affects us and those closest to us, but is also deposited in the overall collective consciousness of the planet.

MASS THINKING

Because our individual thinking affects the planet, we must be responsible for what we think. The mass thinking of religion, however, aborts and takes away our individual responsibility. Many religious leaders do not want us to realize that WE can make a difference. Instead, they invite to join a church with millions of members who can make a difference. Generally, these organizations with hundreds or thousands of members are controlled by an elite few, regardless whether the group is religious, governmental, corporate etc. The bottom line is a select few people always control mass thinking.

For example, joining the Democratic Party puts us in the mass democratic political consciousness of this society. If we join the Republican Party, we become part of that mass political thinking. Just saying, "I'm a Democrat," automatically puts us into the mode of being a Democrat and eliminates us from being an individual thinker. Being a Democrat is not about us as individuals making choices. They don't let us choose whom we would like to have as President. The Democratic Party has already decided what options they are going to present to make us think we have a choice; but we are really just choosing their choices.

Furthermore, the programming of our families to become Democratic or Republican may blind us to the option of making a more educated or enlightened decision based on our own choices. Unless we become aware of our family consciousness, our personal choices evolve only from the mindset deposited by our forefathers. In this manner, the thinking of one generation are passed down to the next.

DISTORTED RELATIONSHIPS

Passed-down thinking sometimes wreaks havoc in relationships as well. Too many relationships today are unfortunately are based largely on appearance instead of spiritual connection. Many couples build relationships and marriage on childhood fables about a prince who carries away a princess to live happily ever after.

FORMATION OF THE BELIEF SYSTEM

We must understand that what happens in our childhood thinking helps to form the way we view our lives unless we learn to shift our perception. What we see, hear and experience becomes the deepest foundation of our belief system. The impressions that happen in the first five or six years of life, are the most impressionable.

Because we heard cute little stories about a prince coming and rescuing the princess and taking her off into the sunset, we expect to grow up, get married, and live happily ever after. When our lives don't turn out like the story, we think something is wrong. We can't seem to separate fantasy from reality. Faulty expectations based on myths generated by mass thinking become the root for much of our unhappiness.

Similar kinds of mass thinking handed down from previous generations have kept women in subservient roles to men. It used to be that a woman would stay in a marriage no matter how badly she was abused. She was conditioned by society or the church that she just had to endure whatever treatment her husband gave her.

BREAKING THE PATTERNS

Things are changing today. People aren't willing to put up with abuse and degradation anymore. They are speaking out, getting help and breaking the old patterns of mass thinking that holds people in bondage. It is about time!

Finally, enough people have begun to awaken to who they are and see something wrong with a relationship that needs a victim and a rescuer.

We are living in a day when we are seeing the downfall of a lot of this mass brainwashing. This is the time when the kingdoms of this world are crumbling to become the kingdoms of our Lord and Christ!

THE WAY OUT—THE ESCAPE MENTALITY

Many of us have thought, or perhaps been taught, the real spiritual answer to the problems of this planet is to leave. Everybody is looking for an escape.

We came to this planet with a spiritual purpose and mission. The purpose is not to come here and end up hating the earth and wanting to leave but rather remembering our spiritual assignment of raising the consciousness of the planet. The minute we start looking at the pain and suffering going on, we want to go back. Deep down at a subconscious level, we start planning our own death, rapture, or some other means of escape, which becomes our hope. This "escape-from-misery" mentality has seeped into the collective consciousness, making us think our primary purpose in life is to leave this planet, rather than to find the kingdom within us.

To me this whole thing seems backwards! Our reward is not to get back into spirit; *we already are spirit.* We *are* love. We *are* joy. We *are* peace. We are here to learn how to become love, joy, and peace in this dimension. We don't acquire love and joy by escaping the planet. We are here as spiritual creations to manifest these realities on earth. The planet is our assignment – it is our laboratory to practice creation – which expands the universe, and hence, source energy.

EMBRACING IS THE ANSWER

Once we start embracing what most religions have taught us to run from, our lives will be different. We will quit hating our lives. If we can change our own perceptions about why we are here, about the world, about ourselves and about each other, we will overcome half of our problems. Stop dreading. Stop running. Stop ignoring. With thanksgiving in the heart, begin embracing the challenges that have been brought to your path.

You have the ability to bring Spirit into the problem. Once we can move into the negatives and find the spiritual opportunity for growth, instead of continually denying and running from them, life will begin to change.

This is what Jesus was about. He was the sample and the example of how to live with our feet on the earth and still be in heaven. He said, "The Son of Man is in heaven," yet His feet were on the earth. He prayed that the Kingdom would finally come here. He didn't pray for everybody to escape, but that the kingdom being manifest on earth as it is in heaven.

PARTICIPATE IN LIFE

As a Son or Daughter, you must become a participator in life. So many "kingdom people" become complacent, sit back and say, "God is going to do it." It is my opinion, if God is going to do it; God is going to do it through us when we start making choices to align ourselves with the rhythm of the universe. We need to spend some time training ourselves to move in harmony with the pulsation of life. We must be the generation whom the end of the age has come upon. We should be the people who stand up and declare life in this human incarnation to stay long enough to raise the quality of life without physical death.

Nothing happens by accident. Every problem, every negative circumstance, is an opportunity to extend unconditional love into the situation and raise it to a higher plane. We are the Sons and Daughters of God, who carry the name I AM. Therefore it is our mission to bring our unconditional love to this planet. We are not here to play the human game. We are here to represent light, truth and love.

Because our perceptions have been healed, we can extend healing to each situation. How can we send love into a situation in which we have hate? By healing our own hate we create space to be filled with love.

By accepting our mission, whatever people say about us will never penetrate us; neither bothers us; and never hurts us. We will never feel anger; we will never seek retaliation; we will always have the opportunity to extend love where there was hate. The more love and light we put into a situation, the less darkness will exist on the planet.

GO IN OUR NAME

Let us go into whatever situation we have been assigned, by focusing on the fact that we are in God's name which is the name, the *I AM*. Let us go and make a difference in our microcosm world. The changes we make to our microcosm are deposited into the macrocosm of the world.

An individual experience of our personal world combines to co-form collective experience. We can make a difference! We can be true to our name! We're not here in Jesus' name; we're here in our own name, which, of course, happens to be the same name Jesus has; the name *I AM*.

COMING FROM THE HEART

INTRODUCTION

After years of having put out information for others to use on their self-empowered journey, I began to emphasize the message of the heart-something each of us desires.

Near the end of the 1980s, while I was under a tremendously heavy anointing, a message came through me during an Easter convention from which the booklet, *God on Assignment* was born. Although, I felt, people never really understood the message of that book, I knew it was a valid message that had to be discerned by the Spirit, not the intellect.

The message of *God on Assignment* is that we are all an aspect of God. A new idea then, the concept has grown into the norm for us now. The understanding was that God created itself to be experienced. It is still all about experience.

If the spirit is to experience this realm of the five senses in which we live, It has to go through the solidification of this zone and materialize Itself. It takes the materialization of a vehicle for the Spirit to move through the material world. If God is to be on assignment in this realm, then the physical body must become the vehicle for the Spirit to travel in the physical world. We can travel in the spirit world in the spirit body, but we have to travel in the physical dimension with our physical body as a spiritual being.

81

David Hulse, D.D.

Spirit agrees to go on assignment with us into many human experiences, to walk through and visit those imprisoned in that experience.

This is why we should prepare, to experience the adventure of coming out of our heads back to our hearts—not for ourselves alone, but for the good of all creation.

THE MEANING OF LOVE

If God is love, then God has a desire to experience love; therefore, God has to have something to love. That is the whole reason behind creation. There is a significant difference however, between what God calls love, and what human beings call love.

HUMAN LOVE

As we experience ourselves in this human realm, we do not really know what love is. We tend to love in degrees. The first degree of love is *Agape* meaning the highest form of divine love, the second degree of love is *Philia*, an affection that could denote friendship, brotherhood or generally non-sexual affection and the third being *Eros*, an affection of a sexual nature. We love our mother differently than we love our dog. We love a tree differently than we love our mate. There are various ways in which we perceive each other with a certain emotion that we call *love*. And this so-called love carries a lot of baggage and conditions from our past. I love you if . . . I love you when . . . I love you as long as you are what I perceive you to be . . .

We cannot love that which is not equal to ourselves. Anything we say we love, but see below ourselves is a form of pity. Anything we perceive above ourselves, we worship or admire, but we don't really love. That kind of love cannot be confused with the love we call our Creator.

For creation to have taken place, God had to create something equal to Itself, *which was* Itself, because that is all that existed, according to Scriptures. Colossians, says before there was God, there was nothing. So, to create meant that God had to extend itself in order to create.

In Christian terminology, we call the God Source, "the Father", and the extension (or expression) of that source we call "The Son". The Father/Mother and the Son are One. *"If you have seen Me, you have seen the Father."* Spirit equals Spirit. IT is still a part of ITSELF. Even though It is not in the same place, IT is the same substance.

All of a sudden, we now have what is called, *This and That*. What this means is now we have *Being (Creator)*, and we have *what that Being has become (Creation)*. We have a Source, and we have a creation of that Source.

GOD-SELF

When God became Its own creation, God experienced Itself, which is what we call the God-Self. What God is, the essence of Man is also. God is spirit; Mankind is spirit, remember there is only one spirit.

INTERPRETATION OF SPIRIT

Fundamental christian doctrine does not teach Man came out of God and, therefore, is God. They believe the human spirit is separate, evil and is in need of salvation. They believe the human spirit is another kind of spirit. Actually, they believe in all kinds of spirits.

Even in the writings and interpretations of the Bible, we see evil spirits and bad spirits, which I feel is just an incorrect translation. When we hear someone say that a person has a bad spirit, what they mean is that person has a bad attitude. When we say things like, "I'm feeling their vibes," we are actually in tune with the frequency of their psyche, where the law of the knowledge of good and evil resides. When we interpret that feeling as negative, we label that a bad spirit. This is what literalist christians incorrectly call a demon or devil, since Spirit is neither good nor bad—Spirit just is. One of my favorite quotes is by Shakespeare in Hamlet *"For there is nothing either good or bad, but thinking makes it so."* I believe that there is one faith, one Lord, one Spirit—One. No matter if it is here or there, it is still One.

The spirit deep within the human experience is the Divine Spirit that dwells within the created. It is between these two entities that there is to be a relationship.

Traditional religion, however, teaches this extended Being, this God-Self, needs to be saved. As a result, we spend most of our lives trying to moralize and make this human good while simultaneously neglecting to nurture a relationship between the God-Self and the God Source. After Jesus, there is not much of a relationship continued between the Father and the Son. It seemed to have stopped with seeing Jesus being the *Son of God*, which precludes an ongoing relationship between father and son in the earth today.

According to fundamental Christianity, the only valid connection between father and son existed between God and Jesus. The rest of us are sinners (bastards) who get grafted in to this wonderful relationship, to have some kind of communion with God through a religious hierarchy.

If, however, we begin from the premise that we came out of God and are forever connected, we can begin to build a relationship. On the other hand the fundamentalist premise that we are separate and apart from God leaves us forever trying to hold on to something given to us (i.e., salvation). In other words, if I am a sinner who receives salvation of Jesus Christ through the Church, I constantly have to be in fear of a created devil, who is always trying to steal my salvation, my joy, and my peace. I then spend the rest of my life trying to hold on to what I already possess, instead of enjoying who and what I am.

Consider the alternative: by assuming we originated our earth experience as a God Self, we originate our journey by whom and what we are not by what we have. In this way, we can build and not be afraid that something will be taken away from us. So, "Blessed are you who are poor in spirit . . ." means we are poor of *having* anything, because we are rich in *being* everything now. We don't have to wait for something to be given later. What we *are* can never be taken away from us. Only what we *have* can be taken. And what we *are* is love.

THE ADVENTURE OF EXPRESSION

VERSIONS OF THE GOD-SELF

The original purpose of creation was to give the God Source a vehicle by which to express Itself and express Itself through the human experience. This is also true for the God-Self. When what we are extends Itself, we express are true being in moments of consciousness. Every once in a while, we experience being love; and because that is what we are, we extend it.

At other times, we choose to extend another version of ourselves based on fear, anger or some other emotion. The beautiful point about knowing who we are is that we can *have* anger and fear, but we can never *be* anger and never *be* fear. Even when we are experiencing the emotion of fear, we remain in our true identity; love. Of course, the more excellent way would be to be love and have love, than to be love and have fear.

Extending anything other than the love we really are causes duality or double mindedness, and makes us unstable. We are unstable, because we do not always recognize and express what we really are. Free will and choice allows us to create something different from what we have been created to be, sometimes resulting in dysfunction. When we create stressful situations, for example, anger, guilt and fear result. Still, the bottom line is that nothing can be taken from or added to what were created to be.

RELIGIOUS CONTROL

Many religions apparently don't want us to know *Who* we really are, because that would empower us too much as individuals. *Who* we truly are does not need a religion. Religious leaders, however, teach that they give us peace, joy, and victory, and that we need them to help us hold on to these things. Our world will begin to change only when we realize that we already *are love, peace, joy and spirit and* we must always come from that premise.

CHANGING OUR THINKING

As humans we do not always experience our true Self. By turning things around in this world we pervert the understanding that we create our world. Therefore, *if we do not understand that we create the world, we let the world create us.* That is a very important statement. We must understand that we are the creators of our world, or the world will create us.

For example, many of us believe that some kind of energy or auric field emanates from our bodies, don't we? We think we create this field from our physical bodies.

Guess what? That is not true.

I believed I created my auric field until a short time ago, when I heard a recording of a seminar speaker asking asking how many people believed their body had an auric field. Almost everyone at his seminar raised their hands. The speaker replied, "That is absolutely incorrect."

We tend to think everything comes from matter. He said that our body does not create our energy field; rather, our energy field creates our body. I knew he was right.

We have had this backwards. We thought the body creates and emanates an energy field; but really, the energy field emanates itself and solidifies itself as a mind-body system materialized as consciousness, which is called the physical body.

THE BAND

Quantum physics is right when it states that concerning matter, we have been wrong, as matter is only energy at a slowed down to a frequency that is perceptible to the five senses. *Therefore there is no matter, only energy.*

Matter is consciousness solidified. Within all appearance of matter is energy in the realm of thought. Behind every physical action, which is an effect, there is a cause. As cause solidifies, it freezes itself within the band of our five senses, becoming slowed down enough for us to experience it, and feel it as being solid. Outside the frequency of the five senses, reality changes.

Spiritual entities around a room do not see things in the room as we see them. They do not see our bodies as we see them. They see atoms made up of electrons, protons and other sub-atomic particles. The things that make us up are the same things that make up everything that is in the physical, material world. That is why Jesus resurrected above the 3-D band. He could walk through walls and change the molecular structure of His body. He wasn't doing anything supernatural; He was doing what people do who live outside the frequency of the five senses.

You and I, however, live in the perception of the five senses, carrying the God-Self within us. It goes wherever we go, limited by the five senses.

THE LOVE RISK

Love took a risk to create. Love always takes a risk. When we fall in love with someone, we aren't particularly concerned about the risk we are taking. We don't know what the future is going to be with that person. We can't predict the outcome of our commitments. We simply hope to grow, and trust everything will turn out for the greater good.

It is no different with the Creator. We play out in the small picture what God played out in the larger picture. When we were created and were given free will and choice, we were told, "You choose, make your own choices, and create your own worlds of perceptions; but remember, you are Me."

THE INVENTIONS OF MAN IN THE WORLD

God has made man upright, but man has many inventions, (Ecclesiastes 7:29).

What have we invented? What comes from us? Most of the time, there is a difference between what comes from God and what comes from us. What is the world, which is the human experience, and how have we used our free will and choice? What do we create? Let's look at it.

First of all, our world that is based on fear. Even our religions are built upon fear. Look at the systems in the world: poverty, sickness, crime, fear, addiction. What are people in our lives dealing with? Alcoholism? Drugs? Nearly everyone knows somebody somewhere, directly or indirectly who is dealing with some kind of major addiction. Millions and millions of drug addicts and alcoholics, who have created their world scenario by the choices they have made.

THE CALL TO RETURN

The God-Self is in the midst of every dysfunctional human behavior. This aspect of the Source always resonates with Itself, even though It does not know exactly where the God-Self has gone, it still remains.

THE MYSTERY OF THE DOUBLE SOUL

As spiritual beings, we are the Soul of God. Feel that for just a moment. When we say we are spirit, our spirit is *a* spirit of *The Spirit*, which equals the Soul of God. We are the Soul of God, but we also have been made a soul. That is why the Bible says we have two souls: the one we are, the spiritual Soul, which is what God is; and a carnal soul, which we have made. The scripture is translated carnally and spiritually *minded* , but if we go back to the original word for *mind*, it is *psuche* in the Greek, which is the word for *soul*. We *are* a spiritual soul, and we *have* a carnal soul. To be a spiritual soul, to be spiritually conscious, is to be spiritually in tune with LIFE. To be very dense and carnally minded is death.

What happened? How did we get carnally minded?

The spiritual Soul went into Adam, but Adam fell asleep and never woke up until the incarnation of the Christ into the man we know as Jesus. In other words he fell into the density of the five senses, and never got out of it. From then on the whole story takes place within the illusion—dream.

THE WAY OUT

When Jesus came on the scene, he started talking about a place that has been translated *heaven, which*, in the Greek, means *elevated place*.

When heaven is referred to as being up there, could this be speaking of a raise in the vibratory frequency of the cellular structure. At one point Jesus told the man that could not walk to "pick up your bed, RISE and walk." The word "Rise" means in the New Testament to collect your faculties. "Faculty" According to the Farlex Dictionary is "An inherent power or ability". In other words as we move into the higher atmospheres of the mind, beyond the range of the five senses, the higher mind will show us the way out, of the illusion of the five senses.

When the scriptures declared Jesus the last Adam, this represents the point in our consciousness of awakening. So, the Day of Christ and It's Coming in us is the day we are free from the illusion of self, to become the authentic Spiritual Self that we were meant to be. "Let this Spirit be upon you that is upon Me," said Jesus. Just before he closed the book on the Old Testament, He read from Isaiah.

"For the Spirit of the Lord is upon Me because he hath anointed me to preach the gospel to the poor; He hath sent me to heal the broken hearted, to preach deliverance to the captives, and recovering of sight to the blind, to set at liberty them that are bruised, to preach the acceptable year of the Lord." (Isaiah 61:1-2).

There it is. Because we have been loosed in earth (body) – we are loosed in heaven (Spirit).

THE IMPORTANCE OF GETTING OUT

Why is it important for us to get out?

We need to escape, from the illusion that we are held in earthly plane only. Religion teaches us that we are held to this earthly domain until something they call the *"rapture"*. That is why God showed us that we are His Soul. The Soul of God is a life-giving Spirit. The last Adam (Jesus the Christ) is a life-giving spirit, (1 Corinthians 15:45).

Let's remember Jesus represents the point at which Adam woke up out of his "stupor" and continued God's plan. In biblical terms "The first Adam *became* a living soul, He got out of the consciousness of the life-giving spirit, which is the Soul of God; and fell into the zone of the living soul, where he lost awareness of the God-Self and became conscious of matter."

Jesus Christ, the last Adam did not come to earth and fall asleep, as did the first Adam – Adam meaning red clay or matter. He did not allow matter to create His world, because of His consciousness, which was connected to the Source. He was able to create the world around Him. In the world He created around Himself, He did not allow death; He did not allow sickness; He did not allow disease; He did not allow limitation; He did not allow lack. In His world, He could pull coins out of fishes' mouths; He could turn water into wine; He could resurrect the dead; He could heal the sick. He was showing us what it was like to be a God-Soul.

All the elements of the world had to obey Jesus. The weather, the earth, the trees, anything humans had invented. Even sickness and diseases had to answer Him when He spoke. When Jesus spoke to someone's epilepsy, for example, it would speak to Him and say, "What have we to do with you? Stay away. Has our time come?"

This is our prototype of what it means to be Fully Consciously Awake.

A PERSONAL JOURNEY

We who are on a spiritual path must know by now that although our experiences are unique to us, they are not for us alone. Nearly everything we experience happens so we can learn for others coming along the same path. When I share my personal journey, it is not only for my own sake, but also for others who may recognize the similarities of their own path.

When I received the Baptism of the Holy Spirit at 16 years of age, I knew I would walk a different path from friends, family and all the hundreds of other people who received the Holy Spirit in Tulsa Oklahoma during that 8 week revival. I knew immediately something was moving me in a unique direction. Some of my friends joined the choir, and others enrolled in Bible schools; but I began to be guided in a unique way, which at that time I did not even understand.

Now I understand that I came here to move through human experiences for the sake of the God-Self. By the late 80s, I knew the God-self as me was on assignment.

I pray this book will help you embrace your own humanity as a gift of God experiencing itself through your human experience!

LWM Message-of-the-Month

THE MESSAGE-OF-THE-MONTH (M.O.M.) is designed to keep you informed of the message flowing through David each month. The LWM Staff picks a 60-minute CD each month that best represents the message of David. This CD is then sent to all who choose to participate in the M.O.M. program. The M.O.M. also contains current announcements of upcoming events and excerpts from upcoming guest speakers. It is an excellent vehicle for you to stay current with David's message between the times that he visits your area.

As a participant, we ask for a minimum monthly donation of $15.00. Many people donate more than 15.00 each month. These funds make up nearly 1/4 of the LWM monthly budget. This program also allows David to travel to new areas of the country in which he plant seeds of hope to new groups. Many times, in the beginning, these groups cannot yet support a weekend with David on their own. Through the M.O.M. David can travel as he is led, allowing these groups to grow.

We encourage you to share the M.O.M. with others as an introduction to LWM. As we raise our individual consciousness, we have a responsibility to extend the vehicles that assisted us to others. The M.O.M. serves as an excellent vehicle for reaching out to others who are searching.

To sign up for the M.O.M. call 800-808-7473 or visit us at <u>www.lightwithin.com</u>**!** We have several vehicles for you to make this donation including Automatic Bank Draft, placing the donation on your credit card or sending in the donation each month in the envelope included in each M.O.M.

We encourage you to become a co-creator with LWM through participating in the Message-of-the-month.

Get the Latest Information . . .

Do you want to stay on top of what is coming through David each month? We invite you to join the Message-of-the-Month. *For a monthly donation of $15 or more, you get:*

- The best of David each month on CD
- Personal message from David
- Special offers to M.O.M. Participants
- The latest schedule information
- Announcements on upcoming events

Call 800-808-7473 or email <u>somaenergetics@lightwithin.com</u> to join today!

About The Author . . .

David Hulse, D.D.
AWAKENING THE BODY OF CHRIST

THROUGHOUT HIS YEARS of spiritual searching, David has challenged many traditional doctrines, theologies and dogmas. He has inspired numerous individuals toward a journey of self-discovery by sharing his own journey.

After receiving the baptism of the Holy Spirit at 16 years old, David was challenged to look again at many of the beliefs taught to him during his fundamental literalist upbringing. David was shown by the Holy Spirit that God's pure word was locked up **in** (inside) the parables for a generation to come who would not walk as their forefathers [Psalms 78], but who would speak these mysteries plainly of the Father. [John 16:25] Confronting the challenge of his childhood beliefs, David wrestled with the emptiness and loss, leaving him angry and anxious about his future ministry.

In the first book in this series, "Take Another Look," he traveled through various beliefs about God, Hell, Resurrection, Sin, Satan, Earth-bound Spirits and Law & Grace. This book, is the next step as he continues his journey understanding the revelation of God experiencing Himself through the human experience. David sees himself as a bridge between the old and the new. Each has a contribution to make to the enrichment of the other. These booklets, which make up this series, were written during his transition. Since very little transitional material is available for those searching, this book has been released to fill that void.

Today David is dedicated to assisting the embodiment of Christ to grow up in every way and into all things . . . to full maturity, building itself up in love. [Ephesians 4:15-16] His stirring presentations of intuitive wisdom will inspire and challenge you to move from believing in God to the experiential realm of knowing God and your co-creative role toward manifestation of the kingdom of God on earth as it is in heaven.